# Clay Target
# Shooting

# Clay Target
# Shooting

PAUL BENTLEY

A & C Black · London

*For Lizzie*

First published 1987 by
A & C Black (Publishers) Ltd
35 Bedford Row, London WC1R 4JH

Bentley, Paul
Clay target shooting.
1. Trapshooting
I. Title
799.3'13 GV1181
ISBN 0-7136-5566-6

Printed and bound in Great
Britain by Biddles Limited,
Guildford, Surrey

# Contents

# Introduction

Clay target shooting has been around a good many years and is at last being recognised as a sport in its own right, rather than as just a means of practising for Game shooting. In fact it is a fair bet that there are far more clay shooters now who do not shoot live targets than those who do.

There are few developed countries of the world where clay shooting of one sort or another is not enjoyed and the number of participants is growing all the time. For instance, in Italy alone there are over one and a half million clay target shooters; the total world wide can only be guessed. In Great Britain, where membership of an association is not mandatory for clay shooters, the number of participants is difficult to assess. Informed opinion, however, has it that the total probably exceeds 150,000.

Clay shooting is divided into a number of so-called disciplines, the three main ones being Skeet, Sporting and Trap. Confusion can easily be caused here, however, when one considers that in the Trap disciplines alone there are four different sub-divisions, one of which, Down-the-Line, has another four sub-divisions! Most of these various sub-divisions are referred to as 'Domestic' disciplines in that they are practised in their country of origin and are not necessarily shot anywhere else in the world.

International disciplines, on the other hand, are exactly that, having rules and regulations which govern the conduct of a competition wherever in the world it happens to take place. Of these international clay target disciplines only two are actually shot world wide. They are International Skeet and Olympic Trap, and these are the two forms of clay target shooting which are featured in the Olympic Games.

Many non-shooters find the Olympics a strange place to have something so seemingly unathletic as shooting. However, the original Olympics were meant to be a test of warlike activities or of those likely to prove useful to the warrior, and there is no denying that shooting slots easily into both these categories. I'm not sure that clay shooting really qualifies, though! This aside, the number of shooting competitors in the last Olympics (Los Angeles) was second only to those taking part in athletics events.

There are four administrative bodies for clay shooting in the British Isles, although England's CPSA (Clay Pigeon Shooting Association) has the largest membership. These associations are open to any shooter or non-shooter who wishes to join and the membership is continually growing. At the time of writing a number of excellent and exciting new developments are being considered, which I think will bring in a large number of shooters who at the moment are hesitant about joining.

There are two ruling bodies for international clay shooting: the most senior is the ISU (International Shooting Union), which controls International Skeet and Olympic Trap, as well as all the international rifle and pistol disciplines shot in the Olympics. The other ruling body is FITASC, which stands for *Fédération Internationale de Tir aux Armes Sportives de Chasse*. This controls FITASC Sporting, a very testing form of sporting indeed, and Universal Trench, a discipline similar to Olympic Trap.

For the person with limited time or cash, clay shooting can be a pleasant Sunday morning pastime spent in the company of friends and finishing off with a pint or two in the pub. There are a tremendous number of small clubs which cater for just this sort of shooter.

For those wishing to be a little more competitive there are events every week throughout the year, most of them having some sort of cash prizes as added incentive. For the dedicated types clay shooting can become a passion which occupies most of their free time (and cash), being every bit as addictive as golf, a fact to which many a 'shooting widow' will sadly attest! Having said that, clay shooting is far from being a male preserve: there are categories for ladies in all the big international events, and the best of the ladies are more than a match for most of the men.

One of the other great attractions about clay shooting is the fact that age has little do do with shooting performance, and there are many veterans who are more than capable of beating the best of the younger shooters. So, any young man or woman thinking of taking up clay shooting can do so confident that, if they enjoy the sport, they can continue shooting long after their contemporaries have been forced to retire from the majority of other sports.

# About this book

Much of what follows has been compiled from my own experience in the guntrade, allied to ten years as a shooting instructor and a similar amount of time spent in international competitions.

I would like to point out, with particular reference to the instructional part of the text, that none of it is intended to be interpreted as being the *only* way, but just one way I have found to be effective.

Furthermore, regarding this part of the text, I take full responsibility for the section on Skeet (pages 78-106), for most of that on Sporting (pages 56-77), but for only part of the Trap section (pages 107-20). For the latter I am indebted to several other shooters who contributed their knowledge by reading and editing the chapter as they thought fit. Special thanks are due to my good friend and GB shooting team colleague, Jim Sheffield, who was largely responsible for the section sub-headed *DTL Technique*.

# 1
# The Shooting School and the Beginner

Taking up shooting can be something of a traumatic experience in more ways than one. The terminology is obscure; finding somewhere to shoot can be difficult initially, and finding out how to shoot can be a bit of a problem to begin with, too. To top it all, it is not exactly a cheap exercise either!

Having decided to shoot, however, there are ways to go about gaining experience which, although at first expensive, save a lot of money and heartache in the long run. After all, the most important thing is to get quickly to a stage where you can shoot well enough actually to enjoy it rather than finding it hard work. To battle on alone for months hoping it will come right is wishful thinking.

The most obvious way to cut corners is to get the advice of a professional shooting instructor, and most of these are to be found at the many shooting schools which are dotted around the country. A course of six lessons at one of these establishments will cost about two hundred pounds, which includes cartridges and clays, plus the loan of a gun if required. At the end of the course the average beginner will have been given a set of invaluable gunfitting measurements, will be capable of shooting in modest competitions or at game birds and, most important of all, will be safe.

Many would-be shooters, particularly men, buy a gun thinking that they are born with some natural inbred shooting ability and that they will soon pick technique up. Sadly, they soon find out that all they have managed to pick up are a number of hard-to-break habits and a great deal of disillusionment. This sort of bad start is the main reason why many people take up shooting, filled with great enthusiasm, only to give up in despair some months later.

It is surprising how reluctant some people are to visit a shooting school; perhaps they imagine they will make fools of themselves, but this should be the least of their worries. Such establishments are intended for every level of shooter, from the accomplished expert, with perhaps only a slight problem on one particular target, to the total beginner who does not know one end of the gun from the other. It is the latter who will make the competent performer of the future, of course.

So the following is what actually happens when Mr, Mrs, or Miss Average books in as a complete novice and invests in a course of six lessons at a decent shooting school.

# Lesson one

Most shooting instructors are affable types who are as keen to see their new charge succeed as the charge himself. Introduction to shooting, then, is approached with care, particularly if the newcomer is a lady or a child, or is obviously rather nervous about the whole thing—as most people are!

The beginner is invariably taken first to a large, steel, whitewashed plate at which the first tentative shots will be fired. Before anything exciting like this happens, though, certain important principles will be discussed. Among these will be such things as gun mount, stance, ready position, how the gun should be carried and many other small but essential details. Most important, and heavily stressed by the instructor, will be the question of gun safety, and this particular aspect will occur constantly throughout the course of lessons until safe, correct gun handling becomes a matter of pride, and something the novice soon comes to observe automatically.

Pupil practising at a shooting school.

This first part of the lesson will usually take at least fifteen minutes, after which the beginner will be asked to fire a number of shots at the white plate on which black marks will have been made as aiming points.

This practice serves a number of functions. It allows the beginner to concentrate on the gun and its handling without having to concern himself yet with an actual target. It also lets him feel what the recoil of the gun is like, a factor about which most beginners harbour grave doubts!

Ludicrous stories about broken shoulders and suchlike are spread by people who have almost certainly never fired a gun in their lives. In thirty years of shooting I have yet to meet anyone who has been injured even mildly as a result of shotgun recoil. Believe me, if injuries were a possibility, 99% of the shooting population would give up today, and I'd be leading the retreat.

The instructor will be watching carefully, though, so that if the beginner is obviously discomforted by the first few shots it is a simple matter to change the gun to one of lesser calibre, if necessary going right down to a .410.

Once the instructor is satisfied that the beginner is ready, he will take him to shoot at his first moving target. It will almost certainly be a fairly slow incoming target about fifteen feet high, not very difficult for the accomplished shot but a fair challenge for a beginner and therefore very satisfying to hit. Most instructors worth their salt will first demonstrate a few shots, after which the beginner will be itching to have a go himself.

After the instructor has explained the technique, the shooter is allowed to fire his first shot at a moving target. Unless the newcomer is an unusually apt pupil, the first ten shots or so will be fired with the gun in the ready-mounted position; that is to say, already in the shoulder.

Whether or not the target is hit does not really matter. What is very probable is that one or more of the targets will be broken before all ten shots have been fired.

The next stage, and this may or may not come in the first lesson, will be to start with the gun out of the shoulder, more likely than not with the stock tucked lightly into the armpit. When starting like this there are invariably a few hiccups as the novice struggles with the problem of mounting the gun correctly, as well as having to concentrate on the target. This is only to be expected. If it were *that* easy, nobody would bother to do it!

After a number of tries one will at last go just right and the target will break. The novice will have broken his first target, having done exactly what a first-class shot would do. If the shooter can string a few of these together, then both he and the instructor will be equally delighted.

In no time at all the first lesson will be over even though, to the shooter, the hour will seem to have gone in about ten minutes.

11

# Lesson two

In this next lesson, ideally about a week after the first, the novice will once again be taken through the basics of gunhandling and safety, although more briefly than in the preliminary hour. He will then be expected to shoot at the same target as before, or a similar one, and again he will probably start with the gun up in the shoulder. This is only at the beginning, though, and soon he will be taking shots with the gun starting in the ready position. Within about twenty minutes he will be at the same stage as he was at the end of the first lesson.

Once these straight targets are being broken successfully (three out of five is a very good average at this stage), the instructor will move on to some close crossing targets, starting with the easier side. For right-handed shooters this is a target which flies to the shooter's left from a point straight ahead.

After a chat about weight distribution and footwork the instructor will again demonstrate a few shots. Some people will wonder about this; after all, they are paying for the ammo! It is perfectly valid, though, and an important instructional aid. Watching a competent shot perform is often more educational than any number of words, particularly when children are the pupils, and I have seen many struggling beginners suddenly transformed by a demonstration of this kind.

Occasionally, the instructor will revert the newcomer to the incoming target again, just to help him regain his timing and confidence. However, it will be just a temporary change, and the crossing targets will soon be tackled again.

The target to the right will be the next thing to be introduced and probably after only a few shots on this one another hour will have ended.

# Lesson three

Once more, basics will form the opening part of this third lesson, after which the shooter will repeat the same targets as in the second lesson.

Most people will begin to feel that they have some idea of what they are trying to do by this stage and targets will begin to break with more regularity. Once the shooter can hit these targets with some degree of confidence, he will find himself being taken to a stand where the targets are a little more difficult.

The next port of call will probably be something a little higher, maybe a low tower throwing a target about forty feet high. The same sequence of instruction will be followed as for the previous stand, with the instructor constantly observing the shooter and making any little adjustments and suggestions as may be necessary.

Surprisingly for the shooter, these targets will often seem easier than those that were first encountered but of course they are not. What has happened is that the shooter has gradually absorbed the instruction and has now taken the first steps towards a degree of competence.

At the end of this lesson the shooter will probably have hit no more targets than he managed in the second hour but the targets will have been that much more difficult.

## Lesson four

By now the instructor will have formed an opinion about the new shooter's potential and will have a good idea of the sort of stock measurements that he will require.

Basics will once again be at the top of the instructional list and the shooter will start briefly on the low targets, move to the low tower and after that probably be asked to tackle something higher. All shooting schools have towers of various heights, although few beginners ever get to shoot at the most difficult of these. The idea is to build confidence, not destroy it! So the new shooter will shoot at targets no higher than about sixty feet, although these will seem quite high enough for most people.

At the end of this session the shooter will find that he has shot twice the number of cartridges that he managed in the first hour, but it is doubtful that he will have noticed.

## Lesson five

At this stage the beginner will begin to feel like a real shooter, and indeed he is. The temptation to buy a gun will be great but it is best to finish the course of lessons and then to take the instructor's advice.

Many beginners, particularly young men, will now want to rush off and have a go at something 'really difficult', but this is just a waste of time and no good instructor will permit such indulgence. Trying to progress too quickly is a recipe for disappointment and failure, as much in shooting as in any other activity.

This fifth lesson is often a resumé of everything done in the previous four lessons, with just a few extras thrown in for interest's sake. Doubles will almost certainly be on the agenda as will the surprisingly difficult going away type of shot.

Shooting instructors are usually somewhat wary men where beginners are concerned, and so it should come as no surprise to the novice if his trusty teacher suddenly seems a little twitchy when he first lets his charge have two cartridges in the gun at the same time.

At the end of this lesson the novice should be starting to feel quite pleased with himself.

## Lesson six

Graduation day at last, when the intelligent shooter will realise that he has been put very firmly on the right path but is only a short way along it. This lesson, like the fifth, will be a resumé of all that has gone

13

before, during which time the instructor will decide on a set of stock dimensions as well as giving his recommendation as to the type of gun which will best suit the shooter's purposes.

And there we are! At the end of six admittedly expensive hours the shooter will have an excellent idea of what he is trying to achieve, be moderately competent on any sort of target and, most important of all, will be safe to shoot in the company of others.

Unless you happen to be a shooting genius, and these are somewhat thin on the ground, don't expect too much from yourself at this early stage. For most shooters, it takes about two years of regular twice-weekly shooting to get to a fair standard of proficiency, and about the same time again to achieve a consistently high standard.

The main thing is to get a good start. Don't play at it for a year or so and then expect a shooting instructor to sort out your tangles. He can and will, but it will take far more time than if you had gone to him in the first place.

## The young beginner

During my years spent as a shooting instructor, one very sad fact was inescapable: well-intentioned fathers are probably responsible for more sons disliking shooting than any other factor! I saw so many boys dragged to the shooting school almost by the scruff of the neck and it is little wonder that few of them showed much interest in the proceedings. Being forced to shoot is no more sensible than forcing someone to have piano or violin lessons. If the inclination is there, fathers will find out soon enough.

In my opinion, the finest way of encouraging a boy to shoot is not to let him! Before a boy is taken shooting he should have been made to go through several pleading sessions until finally he is allowed to accompany his father, but not shoot. Eventually he can be allowed to carry the empty gun, but no more. Later he can be shown how to clean it, how to strip it, everything in fact other than shoot it.

This way, the gun comes to be regarded as something worthy of respect and not just another toy, and shooting begins to be viewed as a privilege and not a right.

Once this happy stage is reached the young man can be taken to a good shooting school and the instructor allowed to do his job. Instructors like nothing better than a 'keen-as-mustard' young shooter but they want him or her to themselves. What they certainly do not want is a hovering father offering misplaced advice and making the young shooter nervous. He will be quite jumpy enough without that!

Is this the best way for a youngster to learn to shoot? In my opinion it's not the best way, it's the *only* way! Young people may learn quicker than adults, but they also pick up bad habits quicker, too. Don't spoil their future in shooting by letting them just get on with it by themselves. It's unlikely to be successful.

# 2

# Guns

If a house and a car are the two biggest investments a person is likely to make in his or her lifetime, then the purchase of a gun can easily rank a close third, particularly if the shooter opts for one of the top quality weapons. It can be somewhat surprising to discover that the very finest clay shooting guns available comprehensively outprice a Purdey or a Holland & Holland, although it is fair to say that seeing such a gun in use in the British Isles would be a rare event indeed! Nevertheless, even modestly priced guns are still expensive and although there are very few badly made weapons on the market it still needs a great deal of thought and care on the part of the shooter before any purchase is made.

To the neophyte or non-shooter a gun is a gun and that is all there is to it, but to the discriminating and serious competitor there is a world of difference between, say, a gun purpose-built for Olympic Trap (OT) and one designed with ISU Skeet in mind.

Before getting too deeply into the whys and wherefores of specific disciplines it would be as well, mainly for the beginner, to examine the various configurations available, along with their respective advantages or drawbacks.

## Side-by-side

The side-by-side weapon the man in the street sees as the 'proper gun', beloved by game shooters, has little practical application in clay shooting and, although occasionally seen at events a few years back, now makes precious few appearances. There is no reverse discrimination in operation here, of course, just lack of suitability for the task. There are a number of reasons for this, not the least being that the vast majority of these guns are made with game shooting in mind, where the gun must be carried all day, sometimes for miles. Anyone forced to carry the average clay gun for more than an hour or two would soon be sorely tempted to throw it into the nearest hedge and leave it there.

The clay gun is built to be the ideal *shooting* weight, which means it is heavy. The game gun, on the other hand, is something of a compromise and therefore is much lighter than the clay version. Because of this only relatively light load cartridges can be used in it, or both the gun and the shooter suffer.

15

Young shooter shooting Skeet with a side-by-side, while instructor Jim Sheffield keeps an eye on him.

Clay shooting rules allow the shooter to use 1⅛ oz of lead shot (1¼ oz in FITASC Sporting) backed up by as much powder as the manufacturer cares to squeeze into a 70 mm case, a combination which leads to high velocities and 'firm' recoil. This is acceptable in a heavy clay gun but not in a game gun.

The question which immediately springs to the mind of the traditionalist is 'Why not just build a heavier side-by-side?' But being light is not the only drawback; there are other reasons for its unsuitability.

From a side view the average side-by-side appears slim and graceful whereas the shooter is presented with an extremely broad 'sighting plane', which makes the kind of precision so necessary in clay shooting difficult to achieve.

The final unwanted characteristic, which eliminates the poor side-by-side from the serious clay shooter's arsenal, is brought about by the very geometry of the gun itself. The two barrels sit considerably above the centre of the stock with the result that, on firing, the gun recoils both backwards and upwards. With the second barrel having to be fired within a split second of the first in many kinds of clay shooting, the undesirability of this sort of muzzle deflection can be readily understood.

Despite all the foregoing, I would love to see some enterprising company create an experimental side-by-side with low-lying barrels in a deep action (to reduce muzzle flip); a ventilated rib raised high above the barrels so that they could be largely ignored for 'sighting' purposes; and, of course, a heavyweight and substantial construction.

Will this ever come about? It seems highly unlikely.

Swedish Ladies' Team shooter, Ulla Samuelson, with a high-stocked Browning over/under.

## Over-and-under

Jumping straight from the side-by-side to the over-and-under takes us in one leap from the least-used gun in clay shooting to that which is far and away the most popular.

The reasons for its popularity are exactly the opposite of those which make the side-by-side so unsuitable, but there are others.

One of the features so often seen on O/Us is the single trigger, as opposed to the twin trigger arrangement of most side-by-sides. The advantage of the single trigger is that the trigger finger does not have to move back in order to fire the second barrel, an obvious aid wherever precise and rapid shooting is a prerequisite.

If the single trigger is such a plus, why do most side-by-sides have double triggers? The simple answer is that the very design and shape of the side-by-side action body makes single trigger construction a tricky and expensive nightmare for many manufacturers. The much deeper bodied O/U, on the other hand, lends itself to the use of the 'intertia block' system, a recoil-activated mechanism which is nowadays highly reliable and relatively inexpensive to produce  The prospective purchaser can rest assured that even in the cheaper guns the single trigger gremlins have long ago been sent packing and the system now rarely malfunctions.

Virtually all O/Us have the raised, ventilated rib which, due to its greater surface area, dissipates heat more efficiently than does a solid one. This is an important point, particularly if shooting in a hot climate.

The final and deciding factor in favour of the O/U is that, regardless of the clay shooting discipline concerned, there are a large number of weapons available which have been designed with that discipline in mind, a fact that will be examined later in the chapter.

## Automatics

The auto-loading shotgun is a popular choice with many shooters for a number of reasons, not least of which is the price. The most costly of auto-loaders are inexpensive when compared with the average O/U, and this is no reflection on the quality, but simply a result of ease of manufacture and a total machine build.

There is a hint of the machine-gun about some of them, while others look as though they have been taken straight from the set of *Star Wars*. This in no way detracts from their shooting efficiency, however, and once one has become accustomed to the 'double shuffle' as the auto-load mechanism comes into play, they belie their rather clumsy appearance and handle well.

One great advantage, particularly for ladies or beginners, is that these guns are notable for their almost complete lack of recoil, a feature of all auto-loading weapons. Thus the neophyte is punished less severely if the gun is poorly mounted in the shoulder, while the more experienced shot can shoot for longer before fatigue sets in. Anyone who feels that fatigue should not be a factor must bear in mind that shoot-offs, often necessary to break a tie for a championship or medal place, can often extend the number of cartridges fired in a day well beyond the anticipated 100 or so. Not long ago a NSSA Skeet championship in the USA was decided only after the two tied shooters had fired over 1,300 cartridges each!

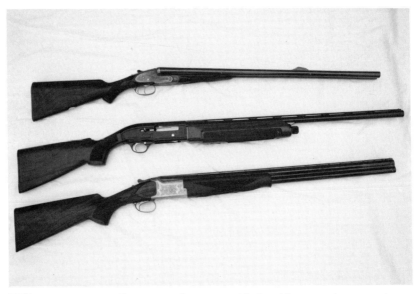

Different gun types. From top to bottom: a side-by-side, a semi-automatic, an over and under.

If these guns are so good, why are they less popular than the O/Us? Their performance is somewhat limited for Trap and Sporting shooting in that, with only one barrel, there is no choice of choke, an important point, although good Sporting results have been obtained with these guns. Another objection to their use for Trap is the cartridge ejection system which throws the spent cases sideways at the next shooter: not a recommended procedure if the shooter is interested in remaining popular with his immediate neighbours.

They are particularly popular for Skeet, however, where different chokes are not required, but all autos have one failing which makes many shooters steer clear of them: they have a tendency to break down, usually at the most inopportune moment. In ISU Skeet, breakdowns can cost targets and so a common sight, whenever an auto user appears, is to see him carrying two or even three of the things as a hedge against the dreaded malfunction.

To redress the balance, however, it must be mentioned that in the last eight years I have seen two Skeet World Championships won with the ubiquitous 'Remington 1100' auto, as well as World and European Championships won with the same weapons. No bad record!

Top Great Britain Skeet shooter, Ken Harman, uses a popular automatic Remington 1100.

## Pump guns

Very similar in appearance to the auto-loader, these guns are quite popular in the USA but are seldom seen elsewhere.

The second cartridge is reloaded by moving the large fore-arm back and forth. Whilst this movement becomes absolutely instinctive to those familiar with the system, it *is* an extra movement to worry about.

Costing about the same as the auto-loader, the pump gun has no practical advantage other than reliability and the fact that in the right hands it can be made to fire a series of shots quicker than *any* other type of gun. (Simultaneous discharge of double trigger guns not included, of course.)

This particular feature has no real practical application in competition shooting although trick shooters do perform some amazing feats with these weapons. This aside, it is not likely that the weapon will find a niche outside the USA.

Outside the scope of this book is the undeniable fact that these guns can be relied upon to function in the most unfavourable conditions, such as are commonly experienced when wildfowling. No one in his right mind will take an expensive gun on an inhospitable foreshore, as salt spray can do some terminal damage to the insides of such weapons.

Although it is not to be recommended, many a pump gun has been stuck barrel first in the mud when a shooter has had to make a quick departure owing to a rapidly incoming tide. If it has been buried deep enough it will still be there the next day and a strip down and clean will soon have it in working order again. Hardly the sort of treatment an O/U or side-by-side would relish.

Having examined the various types of weapon available it is now time to move on to guns intended for specific disciplines.

In Great Britain there are so many forms of clay shooting it is a little confusing, not only to the beginner but even to some quite experienced shooters. A quick count suggests at least twelve different disciplines, although some are admittedly off-shoots of others.

While it is quite possible to shoot all these various disciplines with one gun it must be said that no one with serious aspirations would attempt to do so, the requirements of Trap, Sporting and Skeet being quite different.

## Trap

Down-the-Line is a purely domestic discipline which nevertheless has a large number of devotees. Although some international shooters like to scoff at DTL and say it's easy, they forget that however easy a discipline may be in terms of possible scores it is no easier to win than it is in any other discipline!

The DTL targets rise from a trap 16 yards in front of the shooter and fly away at a variety of unknown angles within certain fixed limits. The targets can fairly be described as steady rather than fast, and few shooters are going to find their reflexes unable to cope. What is required is a smooth, controlled movement, with no hint of hurrying, and the gun for this discipline must be selected with these characteristics firmly in mind.

The right gun for the job will be on the heavy side. around 7¾-8 lb, and will be an O/U with barrels of 30-32 inches in length, choked half in the bottom barrel and three-quarters in the top.

Many DTL shooters will use more heavily choked guns than this but really they are handicapping themselves, particularly with the modern type of ammunition. Through a full choke barrel such ammunition throws a very tight shot pattern which, at the ranges involved at DTL, are just not necessary.

The stock dimensions for a DTL gun are unique to this discipline in that the configuration is deliberately designed to throw the pattern high so that the shooter can see the rising target over the gun as he shoots. Seeing such a sight picture with a flatter shooting gun would almost certainly mean that the pattern centre would be low enough to cause a possible miss beneath the target or, failing that, with the same weapon, the barrels would have to 'blot out' the target in order to shoot high enough to centre the pattern on the target. Neither of these alternatives is particularly desirable. (See also Trap Shooting on page 116.)

Although it is true that all Trap guns need a certain amount of built-in high shooting, DTL stocks feature the highest combs because the DTL shooter has no low targets to contend with. (All the international disciplines do have low targets as well as high.) Many DTL guns have so-called Monte Carlo style raised combs which permit a natural head position as well as making the gun shoot higher than would be true of, say, a Sporting or Skeet gun.

A great many Trap guns these days have exaggeratedly high stocks and these can be very difficult to shoot, so take care when buying.

Full pistol grips are almost a standard feature on most clay guns and DTL is no exception. Unfortunately, some of them are so substantial they might easily have been designed for supermen. People with small hands should select with care, as being lumbered with a big, crude pistol grip is a definite handicap and it is one of the areas of the woodwork department in which worthwhile adjustment can only be effected after major surgery of the expensive kind. (See the chapter on Gun Fit on pages 37-43.)

A rubber recoil pad completes the stock picture, although I would be tempted to remove and drop into the bin some of the misshapen affairs which adorn certain new guns.

There are several independently produced pads, mostly from the USA, which are excellent and which cost relatively little to buy and fit. Some of the more exotic versions are adjustable for pitch and cast, but I tend to think these contraptions are more useful for the hours of happy tinkering than for any practical application. Still, some people are inveterate equipment buffs and are loved, of course, by the manufacturers!

Down at the business end of the gun the raised ventilated rib is practically universal. The width of this vital piece of the gun varies from very slim to extremely wide, although I think the latter eliminates one of the major features of the O/U: its potential for precision shooting.

Most shooters opt for a rib of around the ½ inch mark with a file-cut finish to reduce glare on sunny days. 'File cut', by the way, refers to the appearance of the finish, which is similar to that of the working side of a file. It is certainly not produced by *using* a file!

Many DTL guns have two beads; the usual one at the muzzle and another halfway down the rib. An American idea, these are intended to be aligned so that the muzzle bead sits on top of the mid bead, forming a figure eight. However, as in all forms of shotgun shooting, the target must be the object in focus, never the gun or any part of it. It follows then that neither the front nor the mid bead should be too glaringly obvious or they will attract the eye.

The actual barrels themselves undergo a certain amount of distortion during DTL shooting, particularly if the gun concerned is owned by one of the better shots. The reason is that with the bottom barrel only being fired it is this which tends to become hot and thus expand. Whether or not this is a real problem which affects shooting performance is difficult to tell, but it is a feature of some of the more expensive guns that they have no side ribs and the barrels are joined only at the breach and muzzle, the latter with a floating connector which permits independent movement of the two barrels. Even if this feature does not serve any particular purpose in cold conditions, there is no denying that in a sidewind the ribless barrels are much less affected by gusts of wind than are the standard types of barrel.

Fore-ends come in a variety of shapes and sizes, some manufacturers offering a large choice for any given gun at no extra cost. Unfortunately, this service tends to apply only to guns in the expensive class. Telling a beginner to select a fore-end which feels comfortable is not much use as just about any of them will seem acceptable. The answer here is to be guided by the owner of the gunshop, a breed of person usually far removed from the backstreet car dealer, and who is almost certain to be someone who is as enthusiastic about shooting as is his customer.

Good trigger pulls are a department of gun manufacture that no machine has yet been able to take care of unaided, a degree of skill and feel being required which no machine can adequately duplicate. This means hand-finishing by a skilled craftsman and is why all but the most expensive guns have only reasonable, not good, triggers.

The vast majority have a degree of sprung-loaded slack in the trigger, which has to be taken up before the inertia block engages the sear. While a minute amount of slack is necessary to ensure that the block actually *does* engage, it ought to be almost indiscernible in use. It is possible to have the trigger slack tuned out altogether, but I think this is only really suitable on guns with detachable triggers as these can be kept super clean. Any unwanted dust in a totally slack-free trigger can stop it working, a situation which in a non-detachable trigger would spell trouble.

All the foregoing only applies to guns which employ the 'inertia block' system. Some others, like the sidelock O/Us, employ a different system which means that trigger slack is avoided. Unfortunately, such guns are among the most expensive available.

Regardless of the system, the actual pull weights should be the same, although they seldom are. The actual poundage at which the trigger should 'break' is around 4 lb, and this must happen with a sudden snap, similar to breaking a glass rod, any drag being undesirable.

Trigger creep is a common problem on many guns, but if an otherwise perfectly good gun is found the answer is to trace a good trigger man and have him sort it out properly. This is definitely not an area for the DIY enthusiast!

Do good triggers make that much difference? If having the gun go off at precisely the moment intended has any bearing on the outcome, then the reply must surely be 'Yes!'

Flinching is a problem which seems to afflict some Trap shooters to the extent that they find themselves quite unable to pull the trigger, the eventual shot being the result of a desperate lunge and heave that invariably sends the shot charge anywhere but at the target. To combat this problem the Americans invented the release trigger, wherein pulling the trigger sets the lock mechanism and firing is simply a matter of releasing the pressure. There are a number of variants available; one fires the first barrel when the trigger is released and fires the second when it is pulled again, while another requires that the shooter pull and release for both shots. Personally, I would find these devices the quickest way to the psychiatrist's couch but other people use them, some very successfully.

Of course, the kind of flinching we are talking about here is far removed from the defensive flinch quite common to beginners, especially ladies and children. They pull away from the gun, shut their eyes out of a feeling of self-preservation, and quite reasonably object to the anticipated clout from a recoiling gun. This tendency soon disappears as the new shooter comes to realise that a shotgun's bark is considerably worse than its bite.

The flinch of the experienced shooter, on the other hand, can sometimes be attributed to the same cause but more often it is brought on by some sort of mental block. Before going on the release trigger trail, though, it is worth experimenting with heavier trigger pulls. This may seem an odd thing to recommend to someone who is having trouble getting the shot off in the first place but it often works, as the triggers then need an almost conscious effort to fire instead of the shot being consigned to a set of temporarily malfunctioning reflexes. (I have run this particular course myself, heavy triggers finally sorting it out; lighter ones made it even worse.)

## Olympic Trap

While the differences between DTL and OT guns are structurally superficial, they are nevertheless significant. These differences are brought about by the substantially faster targets of OT as well as by the considerable variation in the elevation of the various targets.

The faster target means that for the second shot (which, unlike DTL, counts the same as the first) the target can be a considerable distance away, leading to a too open shot pattern with any choke other than full. The target also travels further than in DTL before it is seen and reacted to, and once again the lower barrel needs that extra degree of choke, around three-quarter to full being the most popular.

Since the OT targets vary in elevation between virtual daisy cutters and those steeply rising, a built-in degree of high shooting is not greatly favoured. The typical OT stock, then, tends to shoot somewhat flatter than its DTL counterpart.

The actual weight of the OT gun is really a matter for the individual to decide, the important point to remember being that a light gun, while handling quickly, is likely to be more difficult to control. Also, hand-in-hand with lightness comes an increase in perceived recoil, a significant factor in OT where the second barrel is used far more regularly than in DTL.

Barrel length is again down to personal preference although, of course, the choice of eventual barrel length must be based on several factors and not purely on cosmetic appeal. The first is that the shorter barrelled gun will tend to be on the light side, while the longer barrelled one will be somewhat heavier. If this is not the case, i.e. two guns of different barrel lengths weigh the same, the longer barrelled gun will handle more slowly than the other. What this boils down to is that it is a complete waste of time for a shooter with relatively slow or untrained reflexes to buy a long barrelled gun, and *vice versa*.

People tend to ape the more successful shooters where equipment is concerned, hoping that some of the magic will rub off on them. While this is a happy trend for the manufacturers it is not very wise for the shooter, who would be better advised to find what suits him best and then stick with it.

## Skeet

Skeet, unlike the Trap disciplines, started off as a means of improving field shooting but has gradually evolved into a number of separate forms which, nevertheless, use exactly the same layout.

In spite of the differences between the forms one thing has remained common to all: the range of the targets. All are relatively close, the longest being no more than about twenty-five yards, the closest six or seven.

The sort of choke arrangement needed for this type of shooting is exactly the opposite of that for Trap. As wide a pattern as possible, consistent with even pellet distribution, is the requirement of the Skeet barrel. True cylinder or similar is all that is required, although to call any gun with this choking a Skeet gun is often quite wrong as the chokes are only a small part of the whole.

### English Skeet
This is a domestic discipline which has changed considerably over the years. It is probably unique among the Skeet disciplines shot around

the world in that it now does not utilise all of the available stations, station eight having been left out. Quite why this should be I don't really know, but by not shooting this station two of the most spectacular of the Skeet targets have been eliminated, an awkward double on station four having taken their place.

The targets for English Skeet are thrown a distance of 55 yards, which means that they are quite slow. The type of gun ideally suited for this sort of Skeet shooting will shoot to point of aim rather than high like a Trap gun. The weight should be between 7¼-7¾ lb with barrels 27-30 in long.

Because the 'ready' position is optional (you can start with the gun ready mounted if you want to), gunmounting presents few problems and as a result some sort of rubber recoil pad can be used with advantage.

The same observation about short barrels applies as much to Skeet as it does to Trap; the shorter they are the more difficult the gun is to control. Speed of movement is not a requirement when shooting English Skeet and the ideal gun will have built-in steadiness rather than fast handling qualities.

The stock dimensions, then, should allow the shooter without adjustment to shoot exactly where he is looking, rather than high. This is the same as the sort of dimensions found on many guns intended for Sporting clay shooting and it is not unusual for people to use the same gun for both disciplines. It has been made easier in these days of interchangeable chokes, since a half and three-quarter choke Sporting gun can, at the twist of the right tool, be converted into an open-shooting Skeet gun. The observations about triggers apply as much to Skeet as to Trap; they must be crisp and around the 4 lb mark.

For those who shoot the American NSSA Skeet all the foregoing applies, with one or two additions.

The American domestic Skeet used to be the format under which English Skeet was shot a few years ago. Although the latter has now changed, some say for the worse, NSSA continues to use all eight stations on the Skeet field. This form of Skeet is shot mainly in the USA and Canada, but it still enjoys a measure of popularity in Great Britain as it is shot at a number of US military bases around the country.

Like English Skeet, the individual targets are neither fast nor particularly difficult but the problem of beating the opposition remains the same! Although only one shot per target is permitted, as in all the other forms of skeet, 100 straight is probably shot more frequently at NSSA Skeet than in any of the other forms, leading to some prolonged shoot-offs.

The Americans, showing some wisdom, prefer their domestic clay target disciplines to be games in which all members of the family can participate with a fair chance of success, so that although sometimes huge scores are recorded by the experts, the rules have remained unchanged for years.

The only attempt to limit the free scoring at tournament level has been the introduction of a slightly faster target. These now fly 60 yards instead of 55 but this has made little, if any, difference to the good shooters.

Far more effective a means of curbing high scores is the use of four different calibres of gun: 12, 20, 28 and .410, the last two smaller gauges giving even the best Skeet shots something to think about. 100 straight in the 12 gauge competition hardly rates a mention in one of the big US tournaments; such a result will merely ensure the shooter's place in the inevitable shoot-off with quite a few others. The same score in the .410 class, however, will usually guarantee an outright win.

The only limiting factor in the four gun idea is finding the means of paying for the four guns. Fortunately there are ways round this problem. One is to use four auto-loaders (or the similarly-priced pump gun) which are relatively inexpensive; the other is to use the basic 12 gauge kitted out with a set of barrel tubes. These things have long been perfected in the USA, enabling 20, 28 or .410 calibre tubes to be slid into the 12 gauge barrel (only one at a time, of course!) and at once you have a smaller calibre gun which feels exactly like the familiar 12 gauge.

## ISU Skeet
This is the international form of Skeet which is governed by the rules formulated by the International Shooting Union (ISU). The ISU administers both ISU Skeet and Olympic Trap, and supervises all major international competitions throughout the world.

There are a number of significant differences between the domestic forms and ISU Skeet which have resulted in guns so specialised that in some cases they are not much use for anything else. Such guns have their chokes adjusted in such a way that they throw very open patterns, and these are only suitable for close-range work.

Many shooters think that ISU Skeet is something quite new, but in fact it is very similar in format to the way that Skeet was shot in the USA when it was first invented back in the 'twenties and 'thirties. The US NSSA Skeet has gradually evolved from that original formula to produce something much easier and more suitable for family enjoyment.

The rules of ISU Skeet, which are complex in the extreme, make it and the domestic forms related only by the fact that they utilise the same actual layout.

Target speeds are greater at ISU Skeet, the flight distance being 72 yds instead of 55 yds as in English Skeet. Although this may not appear much on paper, it actually makes the target considerably faster.

The address position is also controlled by the rules and they demand that the stock be kept at hip level until the target appears, a somewhat unnatural position which can cause all sorts of problems to the newcomer (and to quite a few experienced shooters, too).

The targets themselves are released by a random and unreadable timer which is activated the instant the shooter calls for the target. The target can then come any time from immediately, up to a maximum of three seconds later. While three seconds does not sound long, it can seem an eternity in the heat of competition!

The guns for this discipline must satisfy a number of requirements. First of all they must fit the shooter in a way which will be enlarged upon elsewhere. (See Gun Fit on page 37.) They must not be light, quite the opposite. They are preferably slightly muzzle heavy, although this must not be carried to ridiculous extremes. The chokes need to be as open as possible, consistent with the pattern holding together sufficiently to break the target at a maximum of twenty-five yards.

There are a number of guns available with 'Tula' or 'retro' chokes, two names for the same thing—a type of choke which throws a wide pattern in combination with an elongated shot string. This is excellent for all types of Skeet, although it does render the gun unfit for much else. (They make great Snipe guns, though, if you can bear the weight!)

Some of these purpose-built Skeet guns come with Monte Carlo-style stocks, more usually found on Trap guns, and these are successful in assisting a shooter who suffers from a tendency to drop his head down to the stock, rifle fashion. They are particularly useful for shooters with long necks, too. The raised comb also encourages a more upright shooting stance than is possible with the more usual type of stock, and for the Skeet shooter who favours this style the Monte Carlo stock is often the answer.

The typical pistol grip is, in my opinion, too full in that it puts the hand under considerable tension when the shooter is at the ready position (gun on the hip), owing to the position which the wrist is forced to assume. This tension relaxes as the gun is being mounted, which means that the gun is held rather loosely just at the moment when it needs to be under firm control.

The half pistol grip is better. It allows the wrist to be relaxed when at the ready position and yet gradually causes an increase in tension as the gun is mounted. The result is a firm but unconscious grip at the moment when it is most required, as the gun is fully mounted and then fired.

The so-called anatomical grips which have appeared in the last few years are of doubtful benefit. If anything, these palm bulges in the pistol grip over-fill all but the largest hands and it makes control difficult, surely not what is wanted. Fortunately, they can be hacked off an otherwise satisfactory gun.

One of the most important features of an ISU Skeet stock is some sort of non-slip pad on the butt, preferably a thin piece of rubber (¼ inch is enough), the sides of which need to be lacquered or taped-up to prevent the edges dragging on the shooting jacket as the gun is being mounted. Ordinary plastic adhesive tape is the material.to use, applied intelligently so that the act of mounting the gun does not snag it so that it immediately unravels. Suggesting the use of tape may cause a few eyebrows to be raised in gunmaking circles but it does the job and does not come adrift in the wet. For the more flamboyant types this tape can be obtained in a variety of colours, although most of us will probably settle for black.

The thing that this pad will do is to locate immovably the gun in the shoulder, even if it is poorly mounted. It may seem a strange thing to advocate but in fact it is possible with experience to somehow manoeuvre a poorly mounted gun onto the target with a good chance of connecting. Even the very best shots sometimes make errors in this department. If such a bad gunmount occurs at the beginning of a double, hitting the first target is a distinct possibility, but without the rubber non-slip pad the gun will almost certainly slip completely out of the shoulder as the gun recoils, making success on the second target highly unlikely.

A rubber pad, then, can be a very cheap way of 'buying' targets.

Triggers set around 4 lb and crisp are the requirement at Skeet, the same as the other disciplines. It is possible to tune good triggers to hold a pull weight of as little as 1½ lb without the dread double discharge occurring, but the advantage of such a light trigger is debatable. I tried this pull weight for about eighteen months and ended up with a flinch that was horrible to behold, so beware!

Barrels for Skeet come in a variety of shapes and sizes as well as having certain features not found in the guns of the other disciplines. The chokes have already been mentioned, although these are sometimes used in conjunction with carefully positioned muzzle slots which have the effect of reducing recoil and in some cases eliminating upward muzzle flip. The latter feature makes for very stable shooting on doubles, since the muzzle disturbance on the first shot is minimal. It might be thought that such devices would be useful in Trap and Sporting but I have not seen one used in the latter, and at the moment they are illegal in the former.

The type of rib preferred is a matter of personal taste although, as with any other guns, the ultra wide ribs are best avoided. No mid bead is desirable as any sort of conscious lining up is not possible or required. For the same reason any sort of large, or worse still fluorescent, front bead should be unscrewed and thrown in the bin to be replaced with something less conspicuous. These targets are difficult enough without great glowing blobs flashing about in front of the eyes! As with Trap, there are some Skeet guns available which have no side ribs, which can be advantageous in a strong wind as the barrels are far less susceptible to air pressure.

Lastly, on the subject of Skeet barrels, there are muzzle weights, the use of which is intended to stabilise the swing and prevent a jerky start when the target appears. Strangely enough, despite the speed of the targets, experienced ISU Skeet shooters often find that they themselves move too quickly and thus lack the necessary control required for consistent scoring. This can be simply that the overall weight of the gun is insufficient for the shooter in question, in which case the solution is obvious. However, should a shooter find it difficult to swing smoothly and yet feel he is already using a gun as heavy as he wishes to shoot comfortably, then it is worthwhile experimenting with muzzle weights. Because these can be attached right at the muzzle end of the barrel, very little weight is necessary to make its presence felt, with instant results guaranteed. (But not necessarily good ones!)

The best method is to approach such modification in easy stages or the gun can be made to feel very strange indeed and practically unshootable. While this can, of course, be instantly rectified by simply removing the added weight, it wastes a lot of time and ammunition, something which can be avoided if the modification is carried out intelligently.

There are some purpose-made attachments for just this very job, although it is possible to buy adhesive lead tape from golf professionals which is very good. Just plain lead held on with adhesive tape will do for experimentation but do not rely on it staying there for ever: use it as a guide for ascertaining the ideal weight, then get the job done properly.

Knowing when the weight is absolutely right is difficult to judge exactly but it should only take a couple of sessions to come close, much of which can be done without firing a shot. The fine tuning can then be carried out on targets, gradually adjusting until it feels right.

When the job is done properly, the shooter will find that the gun swings more smoothly, cannot easily be made to jerk-start, and yet is still not making the shooter struggle on the second targets of doubles.

## Sporting

Sporting clays can be anything the shoot organisers care to present to the competitors, so that despite being named 'springing this' or 'driven that', the Sporting target can legitimately be anything which the traps are capable of throwing. This means that a target as close as a station eight Skeet target can with justification be called a 'Sporting' clay, as can something right on the very limit of full choke range.

The ideal gun for shooting Sporting clays, then, has to have the versatility of the typical game gun, which means that unless the shooter can afford (and is willing to carry) a battery of different guns with him as he moves from stand to stand, the ideal weapon is something of a compromise which falls midway between a Skeet and a Trap gun. In FITASC Sporting the multi-gun option is disallowed altogether.

Close targets suit a Skeet gun perfectly but that same gun is going to be somewhat pushed at ranges over thirty yards, particularly when taking on the smaller targets now permitted even in English Sporting.

The same problem applies to the Trap gun, only in reverse. The steady swinging, tightly choked gun is all right for those long-range targets but becomes a distinct handicap close in.

Probably the ideal solution for English Sporting shooters is to use one of the number of interchangeable choke guns now available. These can be changed from improved cylinder to full choke and anything in between just by changing the choke tubes. However, they do not appeal to those who prefer their guns made in the traditional mould, and so the middle road for the single-gun user would be a gun with three-quarter choke in the top barrel and quarter choke in the lower.

Depending on the type of ammunition used, it is possible to achieve a variety of pattern densities with the same choke on any given barrel. With careful experimentation with cartridges the fixed choke gun can become a great deal more versatile than it would first appear.

The same remarks regarding ribs, stocks and triggers apply as much to Sporting guns as to Skeet and Trap. The actual stock dimensions should be nearer those of Skeet than Trap, although it should be remembered that the one-only Sporting gun has to satisfy a number of quite variable requirements, so the answer is to experiment.

The weight of the gun needs to be at least 7¼ lb, both for steadiness of shooting and to be able to handle the recoil of competition ammunition, particularly in the case of FITASC Sporting where mighty 1¼ oz loads are permitted.

## The gun manufacturers

Asked 'How much does a gun cost?', the knowledgeable shooter can be forgiven if he laughs and says, 'How much have you got?' A high quality Italian 'Fabri', for instance, will damage the bank account by about the same amount as would a top sports car, whereas at the opposite end of the gun spectrum a quite decent weapon may be acquired for the same price as a reasonable video recorder.

In between these two extremes is a vast array of guns to suit all tastes and requirements. Like most things, of course, you only get what you pay for and buying a cheap gun can be a false economy.

For someone taking up clay shooting as a purely casual pastime with no thoughts beyond a few Sporting clays on a Sunday morning, the cheap gun is the obvious choice. For someone with higher ambitions, however, it is worth looking around and maybe spending a little more than was originally intended just to get the right gun.

Many guns are highly priced mainly because of their inherent quality and partly because they have a number of features not found on cheaper guns. Interchangeable locks are a good example. They can be pulled out of the gun at the touch of a button and replaced with another in seconds—assuming that you have one! These units are expensive, as much as some guns, so remember before getting carried away by this particular attraction that you will have to spend more hard earned cash before you get your second trigger assembly.

Such easy access is very useful if the gun breaks down in the middle of a round. However, the triggers of most O/Us can be got at simply by undoing the retaining bolt and removing the stock. Having said that, I must admit to having used for years a gun with detachable trigger capability, complete with two spare trigger assemblies just in case. These are a great psychological support against the day the original trigger assembly gives up the ghost. So far, however, it never has!

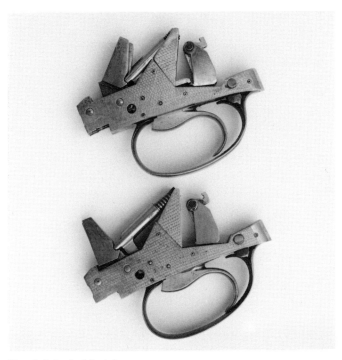

Hand detachable triggers.

Other guns have such features as adjustable trigger positions, lockable safety catches and barrel selectors, as well as oddities such as variable muzzle spacers to alter the relationship between one barrel and another. The thing about these and other adjustable bits and pieces is that, unlike an expensive camera with all its paraphernalia, these pieces are adjusted once and then left in position, never to be altered again. (Except by the inveterate fiddler, who should steer well clear of such tempting equipment!)

These obvious factors apart, what makes one gun cost more than another? There are two major factors involved: quality of materials and quality of manufacture.

Taking a gunstock as an example, it is quite possible for a stock blank of best quality and beautifully figured walnut to cost a great deal of money, and that is before any craftsman starts work on it.

Barrel steel is generally of very high quality and obviously needs to be. Standard of manufacture is another matter. It is perfectly possible to have a very safe pair of barrels which will handle cartridge pressures with ease, which nevertheless look unattractive and perform poorly. Barrels hand-struck, assembled and bored may cost an inordinate amount but such meticulous assembly guarantees perfect bore alignment, barrel straightness as well as an excellent finish to both the exterior and the bore itself.

The same sort of thing can be said about the different types of actions available, the most visually attractive to most eyes being the sidelock, which happens to be the strongest as well. It also happens to be the most expensive to produce. Once again, considerable hand-building and assembling is required which results in finely-tuned triggers and ease of operation, but further expense.

Engraving, of course, is just the icing on the cake but it is an art form which, tastefully executed, can take the gun beyond the limits of mere function and transform it into an object of beauty. In some cases this can be so overwhelming that it almost seems like sacrilege actually to use the gun for what it was intended!

Can superb materials and build quality really justify the cost? To the manufacturer paying for materials and highly-skilled craftsmen the answer is obviously an affirmative, but how about the shooter? Does a sidelock gun with a beautifully figured walnut stock, superb build quality and attractive engraving actually shoot any better than something costing maybe a tenth of the price?

In practical terms it is very easy to say 'No!' until such a gun is tried. The difference may be slight but it is nevertheless very apparent.

In the shooting scheme of things, every little edge over the opposition helps. As Michelangelo said, 'Trifles make perfection and perfection is no trifle.'

This is as true of shooting as it is of anything else and so it is fair to say that although very few modern guns are likely to prove a poor buy, the shooter should dig as deeply into his pocket as he can, always remembering that a really good quality gun is not just a pleasure to own and shoot, it is also a fine investment.

## Cartridges

Two of the great advancements in shotgun shooting in the last few years have been the advent of the plastic cartridge case and the plastic wad.

The plastic case has not only simplified manufacture, it has afforded the shotgun cartridge a degree of weather-proofing it never enjoyed with the paper case. The plastic wad, particularly the now almost universal 'cup' wad, permits higher breach pressure than was previously possible with the felt or fibre wad whilst still retaining a perfect gas seal and minimal pellet distortion. This, of course, goes hand in hand with higher velocity, a very desirable attribute in any clay competition cartridge.

Previously, Trap cartridges in particular had to be satisfied with relatively low muzzle velocities if there was not to be an unacceptable trade-off in pattern quality. Happily, this problem has disappeared and Trap cartridges now benefit from the same high velocities long enjoyed by the less fussy Skeet shooters, to whom a fast cartridge with its pattern blown open was just what was required anyway.

With this last point in mind, I am not sure about the continued use by some manufacturers of the old felt wad in modern plastic cases. Theoretically, the use of the felt wad will cause a more open Skeet pattern to be thrown than will the plastic wad. In practice this does not seem to hold true. Patterning the two different types of cartridge in the same gun, the results are found to be remarkably similar.

The real problem with the felt wad is that when used in combination with the plastic case, it seems to suffer from the occasional semi-misfire: the cartridge goes 'bang' but with a very distinctly flat sound, which means a poor powder burn or gases escaping past the wad. Either way, the pattern quality from such a cartridge is non-existent. This never seemed to occur when the felt wad was used in the old paper cases. Maybe plastic cases 'give' more as the powder burns and expands, allowing gases to escape past the felt wad and so reach the shot column with disastrous results to the pattern. The plastic wad, of course, is able to expand to seal perfectly the plastic case against such an occurrence.

With such a variety of cartridges on the market it is possible to experiment with the different brands and so find one which suits your own gun and style. Certain makes of Trap ammunition throw markedly tighter or more open patterns than do others and with these the one-gun Sporting shooter can alter the pattern-throwing capability of each of his barrels just by varying his ammunition.

For many shooters, the brand of ammunition they buy will be determined by one over-riding factor: price. Like buying a gun, this can be a false saving, particularly in Olympic Trap or FITASC Sporting where a first-class cartridge can make the difference between a killed or a lost target. Also in Skeet, a sweet shooting and consistent cartridge can make quite a difference to the score at the end of the day.

This is not to say that the most expensive cartridges are necessarily the best. One of the finest and certainly the fastest Skeet cartridge made is in the lower price bracket, while its stablemate, a superfast Trap cartridge, is at the other end of the price scale.

The bright thing to do is to pattern test any cartridge you plan to use and just see what it does. Fortunately no longer in production, a certain manufacturer used to produce a so-called Skeet cartridge which threw patterns that would have flattered a Trap gun, regardless of how open the choke was!

The best course is to test your ammunition before you settle on using it. A bit of careful matching up between cartridge and gun will pay any shooter dividends in the long run. If you are stuck within a certain price range, do not despair: there are some truly excellent cartridges that do not cost the earth. You've just got to sort them out for yourself. Once you have, you will have given yourself another little edge over the others that have not bothered. It's another easy way of 'buying' targets!

# 3

# Equipment

Spending a lot of money on a gun and then economising on the sundry equipment is rather short-sighted. Good equipment can make quite a difference at the end of the day so it is well worth selecting the various bits and pieces with some care.

## Shooting jackets

A good shooting jacket must perform a number of vital functions if it is to be of any real use. Firstly, it must fit properly; not so loose that it can swing about when the pockets contain cartridges and not so tight that the seams are bursting. Being the different shapes that people are, it is impossible for the manufacturers to cater for all sizes, so finding one that fits exactly can take time. The alternative is to have one made to measure and some of the better manufacturers can handle this for you.

For Sporting and particularly ISU Skeet, the shoulder pad needs to extend from the shoulder right the way down to the pocket. This will prevent the stock from snagging as it comes up, something that easily happens with the shoulder-only type of pad. For perfection, the full length pad will feature vertical stitching at 1 inch intervals as this stops the pad from rucking up as the gun is mounted.

Some people do not like shooting in jackets (I'm one of them), preferring something less constricting. While it is quite possible to shoot in anything that takes your fancy, a tight-fitting thin sweater is ideal in all but the warmest conditions. In very hot weather some shooters wear just a T-shirt, but the recoil becomes a bit too obvious when dressed like this! To complete the jacketless outfit a leather cartridge pouch is necessary. This should be capable of carrying at least 30 cartridges.

## Shooting glasses

Glasses perform three distinct functions in shooting. One is target-colour enhancement, two is protection of the eyes from the harmful effects of the sun's rays, and three is protection of the eyes from bits of stray clay target. The latter is a particular and dangerous problem on some Sporting stands and is always present whenever Skeet ranges are used which have been built back-to-back.

Good shooting glasses will cost considerably more than 'sun glasses' as much more is expected of them. The frames on a good pair will be inconspicuous in use and will feature ear clips which are adjustable and which bend completely around the ear, preventing any unwanted movement when shooting. Good glasses will also have lenses which have been optically corrected, an essential factor for shooting, whereas cheaper glasses have their lenses punched out of sheets of plastic and are likely to suffer from various optical aberrations. Basically, this can mean that the target is not where it appears to be be—not very comforting!

Some feature interchangeable lenses which enable the shooter to have a good variety of tints on hand to suit the targets and conditions. A number of glass tints are useful but to build up a collection of all of them would be pretty expensive! Probably essential is the dark grey/green tint, polarised, and suitable for most bright weather shooting if you are not too fussy, and mid-bronze if you have trouble seeing orange targets.

When the light is down, yellow is often recommended, but in fact this tint reduces the amount of light reaching the eye still further. It cannot lighten the darkness as some people claim—no tint can do that—but it filters out the least amount of light (other than clear lenses, of course) and still protects the eyes from the flying bits.

For a reasonable pair of glasses you may expect to pay at least as much as you would for a decent bottle of Cognac and as much as six times this amount for the very best, the six-bottle variety having interchangeable everything and coming from the USA.

## Footwear

Any flat shoe will do provided it does not allow the feet to move about inside. A grip sole is an advantage, too, particularly on some concrete surfaces which become slippery in the wet. Purpose-built shoes are available, of course, some of which are adjustable in all sorts of unbelievable ways. Most people opt for a decent pair of trainers, however.

Ladies must definitely avoid trying to shoot in fashionable high heels, that is if they are interested in shooting a good score. Attractive though they are, high-heeled shoes have no place on the shooting field.

## Hats

At one time shooters favoured the baseball type of hat, the idea being that the peak could be pulled down to shield the eyes from the sun. Whether or not this is a good idea is a matter of experiment. I find that if I pull down the peak I cannot see the target, and that is not much use.

Hats are a bit of a mixed blessing, particularly in hot weather. The baseball type hat gets very hot to wear unless it is well ventilated and for this reason many shooters prefer to wear something like a sun hat with a brim all the way round.

The clay shooter's 'uniform' has changed in the last few years, the general trend being towards clothes that are not only functional, but smart, too. Hats, strangely enough, have not quite kept pace with the rest of the sartorial outfit and there are some rare examples to be seen, some of them full of pellet holes! This is not from an attempt to improve circulation but because tradition has it that those who shoot a hundred targets straight get their hats shot by whoever happens to be about at the time. I am pleased to confirm that this is seldom done while the owner is still wearing it! Perhaps because of this trend, shooters are not prepared to risk having a good hat shot up so they wear any old thing they have got lying around.

Hats, then, are strictly a matter of personal preference, though something with a brim or peak may prevent glasses from being rain-spotted.

## Odds and ends

Besides all the obvious pieces of equipment, there are a few things that all serious shooters will have in their bag when at a shoot. A decent set of waterproofs is essential for line-judging or refereeing, even if you hate to shoot in them. A couple of dry towels to keep the gun dry between stands when it's raining make all the difference to how the gun feels. A spare shooting jacket and a change of clothes can be a great morale booster on a wet day, too. Lots of pairs of earplugs, if you use them, should be dotted about the person; there is nothing more annoying than having to shoot a whole round of Skeet, Trap or Sporting with your ears ringing!

Skeet shooters should always have a stiff steel barrel-brush handy, especially if their guns happen to have retro style chokes or similar. Such chokes quickly become clogged up with plastic and lead and this has an adverse effect on pattern quality. A quick scrub between rounds keeps them clear.

Being something of a pessimist, I always like to carry enough tools with me to strip the entire gun if necessary, as well as a whole pile of spares, although for most people this would not be entirely practical. I must admit that most of the kit I carry about with me rarely sees the light of day. However, when things are getting tense, it is nice to know that it is all there as a back-up should the need arise.

# 4

# Gun Fit

Gun fit comes into the category of fine tuning, which means that it is ignored by most shooters who find they can get along quite well with their gun in original factory trim.

This is an unfortunate attitude because there is no doubt that a well fitted gun can sometimes make a dramatic improvement in a shooter's scoring ability. For someone already at a high level it can swing the balance between champion and also-ran status, often the difference of just one target in a two hundred target shoot, and reason enough to investigate gun fit more closely.

Before going too deeply into the subject it will be as well to define just what gun fit is *not*!

Some gunshops will have you believe that it is possible to obtain a correct gun fit whilst within the confines of their shop, but no gunfitter, however clever, can achieve a satisfactory result without seeing the person being fitted actually shooting. The reason for this is simple: how a shooter points the gun when mounting it in a shop is usually a very different thing from what he does when confronted with a moving target.

Measuring the shooter for a gun by recording his arm length, shoulder width etc. is again of little use as these measurements have only a small bearing on where the gun actually points when shooting, and take no account of how he personally mounts the gun, how he holds his head when shooting or, most importantly, how his eyesight affects the direction in which the gun points.

In a nutshell then: a well fitted gun will feel comfortable; on the other hand, a gun that feels comfortable need not necessarily be a good fit!

## Dimensions

Gun fit falls into three separate but inter-related dimensions: length of stock, of which there are three measurements; bend or drop, of which there are two measurements; and cast, of which there are four measurements. (Normally, right-handed shooters have cast off, left-handed shooters cast on.)

The illustration on page 41 will explain exactly where these measurements are taken.

### Length
Stock length is entirely concerned with ease of gunmounting coupled with firm location of the gun in the shoulder.

An over-long stock is difficult to mount and will regularly get stuck halfway up to the shoulder, or, more painfully, will tend to be forced out onto the biceps or upper arm.

The low mounted stock will cause many shots to go high. This is easily understood if the gun is first mounted correctly and then the stock is dropped slightly lower in the shoulder. As the stock goes down so the muzzles go up.

If the gun comes up high enough but ends up on the arm instead of the shoulder, the muzzles will usually be deflected somewhat to the left (for a right-handed shooter). This is one of the most common faults for beginners.

The too-short stock has various effects. Inconsistent gunmounting is the problem, with the gun ending up in a variety of unintended positions around the shoulder and arm area. Because neither the left nor the right arm is properly extended when the gun is mounted with such a stock, excessive recoil can be a problem.

Few shooters realise just how much recoil is absorbed through the arms. Anyone who does not want to take my word for it could do the following. Rest the fore-end on the leading hand instead of gripping it firmly, then fire the gun from the shoulder while retaining a slack grip with the trigger hand. If you are foolish enough to try this, please load only one cartridge, for the gun will leap about quite alarmingly. It will also fetch you quite a clout and it is not an experiment you will care to repeat.

A short stock has a similar but not quite so violent effect, though the cumulative result is just as unpleasant.

### Bend (Drop)

Bend or drop determines how high or low any given gun will point from an identical gunmount position. Quite simply, a gun with too little drop will tend to shoot high while a gun with too much drop will do the opposite. Of the two, too much drop is the least desirable. In order to shoot where he is looking with a low drop measurement (at the target, hopefully), the shooter is forced to hold his head off the stock and this leads to guaranteed inconsistency. When the shooter does not make this correction, not only does the shot inevitably go low but there is a possibility that the shooter's master eye will lose sight of the target, which will be hidden by the intruding breach of the gun. If this happens the shot can go anywhere.

### Cast

Cast determines the direction in which the gun points relative to the target, the stock ideally being offset just enough so that the master eye is aligned perfectly with the very centre of the rib when the gun is correctly mounted. Owing to physical differences, some shooters will require more cast than others.

For 99% of the shooting population the standard factory cast off of approximately ¼ inch at heel is about right. This includes those shooters who for one reason or another must shoot with an eye closed.

There are a number of conditions familiar to those involved in gunfitting which, while having little bearing on actual seeing ability, seriously affect where certain shooters point a gun when shooting with both eyes open. They are listed as follows.

*Central vision*  This means that the shooter concerned has no master eye as such. If he attempts to shoot from the right shoulder with both eyes open he shoots to the left of his target, whereas if he attempts to correct things by learning to shoot from the opposite shoulder he will then miss his targets on the right. Sounds hopeless, doesn't it? Fortunately, he has two options. One is simply to shut one eye, obviously the left one for a right-handed shooter, or have a gun built in such a way that its stock bends quite dramatically, thus compensating for the degree of unconscious aiming-off. The first alternative is the best and certainly the cheapest. Unfortunately, there are those who cannot shut one eye independently of the other and these people are rather stuck with the bent stock.

*Wrong master eye*  More straightforward than the previous example, this is a very common thing among ladies and children. It refers to the situation where the right-handed person has a left master eye, and *vice versa*. Trying to shoot with both eyes open with this particular problem can result in misses of several feet. This time there are three cures.

One, and simplest, is to shut the master eye.

Two, and not recommended, is to have a gun built with a monster cast. These things are called across-eyed stocks, but whether the title refers to the function or the effect of seeing such a horrible thing I am not really sure! Whichever it is, I personally would not give one houseroom.

The third and best alternative is to learn to shoot from the opposite shoulder, which has several advantages. It is inexpensive, and it brings the master eye into use, whereas shooting with an eye shut cancels this eye out altogether. Most important of all, it permits two-eye shooting.

The catch, unless you are a complete beginner, is that initially scores drop as the shooter struggles to re-learn everything in reverse. However, it soon comes right, and to someone who has never tried it, two-eye shooting can come as something of a revelation.

The ultimate purpose in the achievement of a correctly fitting gun is that the shooter is then able to concentrate fully on the target and not on a number of compensations required to deal with a gun which fits poorly.

## The gunfitter

There is only one sane way for an inexperienced shooter to obtain a good gunfit and that is to visit a qualified gunfitter at a good shooting school. Take advice on this particular point from shooters who are knowledgeable on the subject. The good performers will know who is good and who is not. As in so many skilled trades, there are cowboys in wait for the unwary.

However, having found a good one the result is very worthwhile.

To determine the correct gunfit the gunfitter has three aids: an adjustable gun, a variety of different targets and his own experience. Using the latter he will set up the adjustable or 'try' gun, as it is known, to what he considers to be measurements roughly correct for the shooter concerned. This will be ascertained before moving to the fitting plate.

The fitting plate is a large whitewashed area that has a number of aiming marks, and the gunfitter will watch carefully as the shooter takes several shots, after which he will adjust the try gun as he deems necessary. At the end of a short session here the gun will be a little nearer the mark but certainly not yet dead right.

The first dimension attended to by the gunfitter is the length of the stock. As has already been said, an overlong stock causes the gun to move out on the arm with the result that the shot goes to the side of the target. For the gunfitter to alter the cast of the stock to compensate for this mismount would be correcting one mistake with another. This is why stock length must be adjusted first.

The shooter will be asked to shoot at a number of targets during which time the gunfitter will make slight adjustments until he is satisfied that the length is correct. To do this effectively, of course, it is essential that the shooter wear his normal shooting clothes, for a thick sweater or jacket can make a significant difference to the final measurements.

The bend or drop will have been adjusted fairly accurately on the fitting plate and may well need only a slight alteration, but an important one. Small changes here can make the difference between a smashed target and one which is just chipped or missed.

The cast is decided in the same fashion.

Once the gunfitter has determined the fit within fine limits he will then watch as the shooter fires a series of shots at various targets and will make such minor alterations which he may feel are necessary.

At the end of the session, which will last about an hour, the try gun will be measured and the resulting dimensions recorded.

As a matter of interest, the following is an example of stock measurements taken from a standard off-the-shelf factory-made Skeet gun.

| Length | heel | centre | toe |
|---|---|---|---|
| | 14¾″ × | 14⅜″ × | 14¾″ |

| Cast | heel | face | comb | toe |
|---|---|---|---|---|
| | ¼″ × | ⅛″ × | ⅛″ × | ¼″ |

| Bend | heel | comb |
|---|---|---|
| | 2¼″ × | 1½″ |

These can be readily understood by consulting the illustration.

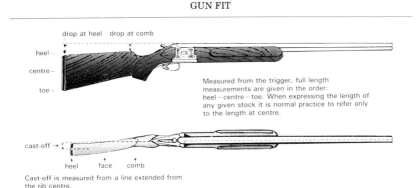

drop at heel    drop at comb

heel –
centre –
toe –

Measured from the trigger, full length
measurements are given in the order:
heel – centre – toe. When expressing the length of
any given stock it is normal practice to refer only
to the length at centre.

cast-off →

heel    face    comb

Cast-off is measured from a line extended from
the rib centre.

Measuring stock dimensions.

The following is an actual set of dimensions taken from the gun of
a world-class Skeet shooter.

| Length | heel | centre | toe |
|---|---|---|---|
| | 15″ | × 14⅞″ | × 14⅞″ |

| Cast | heel | face | comb | toe |
|---|---|---|---|---|
| | ⅜″ | × ¼″ | × ⅛″ | × ⅜″ |

| Bend | heel | comb |
|---|---|---|
| | 1¾″ | × 1½″ |

By comparing the two examples the differences are obvious. Using
a gun equipped with the standard dimensions would soon reduce our
world-class Skeet shooter to the ranks!

This brings us to the specialist gunfit required for the various
disciplines. It is essential that the fitter is advised as to the purpose
to which the measurements will be put. Any given shooter will require
quite different measurements for Trap than he will for, say, Skeet, so
the dimensions cannot be finalised until the gunfitter has seen the
shooter in action at his own particular discipline.

The try gun used for this exercise must be an over-and-under, too,
since the measurements taken with a side-by-side, particularly with
regards to the cast, can be very different.

Once a good fit has been obtained and everyone is happy the
dimensions can be written down and taken away by the shooter who
can then have his own gun adjusted accordingly. This can sometimes
be where problems begin.

Most O/Us have the stock secured to the action body by a long bolt
which passes through the hand of the stock into a threaded bar at the
rear of the action. The presence of this bolt limits the amount that the
stock can be bent vertically or laterally, a nuisance where a large
deviation from standard is called for. Some guns may be purchased
with stocks made to measure at no extra cost, while certain
manufacturers can supply any size or shape of stock (within reason!)
'off the shelf'.

Anyone contemplating buying a gun with this facility available is
well advised to obtain their correct gunfit first, as having to purchase
a second stock could prove expensive.

For those whose guns do not feature such bolt-on luxury, all is not lost. A moderate amount of cast can be obtained by 'sweeping out' an area of wood where the face touches this stock. As much as ⅜ inch of cast can be obtained with such a method and very few shooters will need as much as this.

The left-handed shooter will have long ago probably resigned himself to making do in a right-handed world but this is a big mistake where shooting is concerned. Very few factory-made guns are built with left-handers in mind and this can only mean that the left-handed shooter is struggling with a gun which has a cast that for him is set a good ½ inch in the wrong direction! Once again, the shooter would be well advised to get fitted first, then order a gun that will arrive all set up for left-handed shooting.

Altering the bend is another matter altogether as the stock is a great deal deeper in the hand than it is wide, making any sort of bending up or down a risky proposition. Even if the stock does succumb to the gunsmith's efforts to make it bend, there is no guarantee that it will stay that way. Stocks which have been bent under considerable pressure have a nasty habit of springing back to the original shape.

A method more assured of success is that of simply building up or shaving down the stock until the measurement is right. This is well within the capabilities of anyone handy with tools but if a first-class job is wanted, leave it to the gunsmith to have it done.

To avoid all the hacking and cutting, though, get the measurements first, then get the stock made to measure.

Once the basic fit has been obtained there are a few other small but important factors which no gunfit measurements ever take into consideration. One of the most important is the thickness of the hand of the stock. On many guns this is too large in circumference, making the gun feel clumsy and awkward to control. The acid test is as follows:

Take the gun in both hands, set up correctly, then mount the gun. With the index finger on the trigger, the thumb should be curled around the grip to rest comfortably on the side of the middle finger. (See photo on page 47.) Without any undue effort, this hand position controls the gun far better than if the thumb and middle finger are apart. If this is not possible with your gun, it might be a good idea to do something about it. Having the hand of the gun slimmed down is not exactly cheap since it involves re-chequering afterwards, but if you can afford it it is well worth having it done.

The fitting of a non-slip pad is another essential item for the shooter who finds that the gun moves in his shoulder as he fires the first shot. As mentioned elsewhere, a thin rubber pad is the thing to have, with the sides taped up so that they do not catch as the gun is being mounted.

## Balance

A well balanced gun is usually defined as one which, when supported beneath the cross pin (the point where the barrels pivot), will tip neither forwards nor backwards. This is not a very satisfactory guide since a broomstick with a pound of lead tied to each end can be made to do the same thing and it feels about as unbalanced as some guns!

Balance, then, cannot be so readily defined as simply indicating the moment of inertia: it is rather more subtle than that.

A fine handling gun comes about as a result of good distribution of weight, a combination of a number of related elements, such as barrel weight and taper, barrel length, action body weight and shape, fore-end weight and the length and weight of the stock. Most of these are qualities inherent in the gun's manufacture but they can sometimes be beneficially altered.

Generally speaking, a gun which tends towards stock heaviness will be relatively fast-handling, whereas the opposite will be true of a gun which is muzzle heavy, even though the all-up weight of the two guns may be identical. This can be exploited in several ways.

Ladies or small men can increase the weight of the gun by adding a certain amount of ballast to the stock, thus reducing recoil while retaining ease of handling.

A shooter looking for more stability rather than speed can add a small amount of weight to the muzzle. This trick is particularly relevant for Skeet shooters, the guns for which benefit from being muzzle heavy.

Some Italian-built guns are notably stock heavy and, whereas this can be cured as just described, their weight is often sufficiently high to justify taking away a certain amount of weight from the stock simply by removing the butt plate and drilling out some wood. Do this with care! A surprisingly small amount of wood can make a significant difference to the point of inertia.

The question in many shooter's minds will be, 'Is all this worth it?'

The answer probably lies with observation of the top shooters and their guns. Very, *very*, few use run-of-the-mill weapons and in many cases their guns exhibit signs of some hacking of the amateur kind!

In other words, they have taken great care to ensure that if they are in good shooting condition themselves the gun will give them that little bit extra in the score department. Any shooter using a gun still in its off-the-shelf condition is possibly handing these top shooters a target or two before the competition even starts.

Can anyone seriously afford to give such shooters even one target?

# 5

# Basic Technique

Clay shooting, in common with all sports, has certain fundamentals which must be mastered before the shooter can hope to make any serious progress. The relative newcomer watches the top performers and very reasonably concludes that the whole thing is impossible as there seems to be a thousand different ways of achieving the same result.

Fortunately, this is not so.

Take away the various mannerisms and the vagaries of style and beneath it all is a set of basic techniques which are common to all who shoot well. Style is difficult to define, as well as probably being impossible to categorise, arising as it does as much from a shooter's personality as from any shooting method he may have learned.

As a result, two individuals taught the same basic technique by the same person can easily evolve into two shooters with notably different styles and mannerisms which, beneath the surface, are nevertheless identical.

The following notes may help sort the wheat from the chaff.

## Gunmounting

The deceptively simple act of raising the gun to the shoulder and face is without doubt the most basic and important of all the fundamental techniques.

Good shotgun shooting requires excellent hand and eye co-ordination in combination with well-trained conditioned reflexes. With conscious and deliberate rifle-style aiming being both undesirable and unproductive, it falls to a consistent gunmount to ensure that the gun is pointing where the eyes are looking: at the target.

The actual procedure for practising this vital movement is described in Training Methods on page 134. However, before this stage can be reached it is necessary to learn how to hold the gun correctly. Many shooters, on reading the last sentence, will probably smile and prepare to move on. But I hope they will hesitate a moment, for many quite reasonable shots *do not* hold the gun the right way and they are definitely handicapping themselves.

If good gunmounting ensures that the gun is pointing where you want it to, then holding the gun properly goes a long way towards enabling you to mount the gun correctly in the first place, as well as giving you full control of the gun when it is actually in position. This is of particular importance when two shots must be fired in quick succession, a common occurrence in modern clay shooting.

## The correct hold

Essentially, a good hold on the gun gives firm control without recourse to fierce and desperate over-tight gripping.

With the gun correctly positioned in the shoulder the suggested hand positions are as given below. As usual, this is directed at right-handers. Understanding southpaws please transcribe.

### Left hand

The left hand performs the vital function of pointing the gun at the target and it follows that any undue tension in this hand will make fine control difficult.

Observation of any top shooter will show that the left hand does not support the fore-end with the palm but rather with the fingers. (See photo below.) From the shooter's viewpoint, the back of his left hand faces only slightly down and mainly out to the left side of the fore-end. In this position the fore-end sits principally in the fingers, the thumb and its base, which permits excellent control without too firm a grip being required. With the hand in this position the fore-end actually rests only on the *index* finger. Some shooters like to curl this finger around the end of the fore-end, in which case the gun will rest on the middle finger. With reference to this alternative it should be pointed out that in hot weather the index finger is going to end up rather singed!

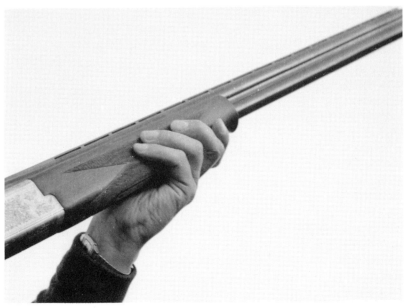

The left hand is placed on the fore-end.

How tight a grip is necessary? It has been suggested that the grip be a relatively gentle one, but the question is 'by whose standards?' A gentle grip from a weight-lifter is scarcely comparable with the gentle grip of a young lady. The thing to bear in mind is that the grip is supposed to control the gun during recoil, so that second shots may be fired instantly without a struggle to regrip the woodwork. If the gun is moving in the hand as the gun is fired then the grip is too weak. When the grip is correct the gun will not move about in the hand at all, with the added bonus that a certain amount of recoil will be absorbed by the left hand and arm, a very desirable situation.

Exactly where on the fore-end the left hand should be placed is open to debate, since good shooters tend to vary on this point quite considerably. Generally speaking, the further back the left hand is placed on the fore-end the faster the gun may be swung, but control is superior with the hand placed further forward. A case of swings and roundabouts!

Personally, I prefer the more forward position. Not only does it permit more precise control of the muzzle, it also absorbs recoil better than when the hand is positioned further back. This is because the arm, with the hand forward, is that much straighter (though never completely straight) and is thus less prone to 'giving' as the gun recoils.

However, this is something for the shooter to decide for himself after experiment. Remember, the further back, the faster you swing but the less control you have, and *vice versa*.

One final point: do not get into the habit of allowing the fingers or thumb to stray onto the sides of the barrels. In our frequently chilly weather it is very easy to go for months without a warm day, particularly from November onwards, and the fingers can sit on the barrels without harm. Come the warmer weather, though, and the barrels become far too hot to touch. Remembering to keep your fingers off the barrels will then be a distraction which will not help your scores.

**Right hand**
As with the other hand, tension is undesirable but firm control is necessary. If the thumb cannot curl around the hand of the stock and rest against the middle finger, then firm control with a relatively light grip is not possible. (See the photograph on page 47.)

For people with small hands it may be necessary to have this part of the stock slimmed until the position is possible without undue strain. Once achieved, however, the right hand is effectively locked onto the gun whilst the actual grip pressure is minimal. (See Gun Fit on page 42.)

The light but firm grip also permits the trigger finger to remain relatively relaxed, essential if precise timing of the shot is to be achieved. It is tension in this hand which can so easily lead to flinching as well as a rather jerky gunmounting movement. If you try tightening the grip of either hand, it can easily be seen that the arm muscles tighten also and this will rob the swing of smoothness.

Right-hand grip.

The trigger finger itself must always sit on the trigger. Gameshooters taking to clays must break the habit of having this finger resting against the side of the triggerguard. The latter is the mandatory position for a gameshooter who frequently carries a loaded gun for considerable lengths of time without firing a shot and it is a necessary safety precaution. However, in clay shooting the gun is only loaded immediately prior to firing a shot or shots from an established safe stand or area. Safety catches are therefore left permanently in the 'off' position (or preferably disconnected altogether) and the finger sits on the trigger.

The part of the index finger which actually touches the trigger is the pad of the finger, not the first joint. All fine handwork involves the use of these pads and they are very sensitive, so why consign something so delicate as precise trigger timing to the insensitive joint of the finger?

Correctly positioned, the right hand will also, like the left, absorb its share of the recoil. Between the two, the amount of recoil the hands take is considerable, making shoulder-absorbed recoil quite minimal. Many a newcomer is amazed when after a few months the recoil of the gun seems far less than it was originally. They fondly imagine that their shoulders have toughened up when what has really happened is that their hands have learned to absorb their share of the recoil.

## Basic shots

Targets can only do three things: go left, go right, or go straight. Of course, there are endless variations on these three themes but the basic technique is the same for all of them.

**Straight targets**

Although in theory the simplest, these targets crop up frequently in all of the clay shooting disciplines.

In Skeet they are encountered on stations one and seven; in a variety of guises in Sporting shooting; and as one of the most regularly missed targets in all the various Trap disciplines!

As this chapter is aimed at basic technique only, these variations will be discussed in detail elsewhere.

**Where to look**

One of the problems experienced by beginners is exactly where to look when waiting for a target to appear.

The answer is to look at nothing in particular, certainly not the gun. Just allow the eyes to hold a soft focus around the area where the target is expected to appear. From this point the eyes will instantly focus on the target as it first comes into view.

**The first few shots**

There is nothing like a bit of early success to keep a newcomer going and to this end it does not do any harm if the first twenty or so shots are fired with the gun already in the shoulder. The gun must be carefully positioned, of course, and after a few shots have been fired the new shooter can then try mounting the gun from the ready position before the target is actually on its way. If he can do this under the watchful eye of an experienced shooter so much the better.

Let's imagine a low target, maybe fifteen to twenty feet high, which will be appearing from behind a hedge and flying rather lazily, directly over the shooter, who is ready and waiting.

The stance should be as the illustration on page 49 shows. Note that the feet are quite close together, with the weight favouring the forward foot. The shoulders are half-facing the hedge, not square or sideways on. This half-facing position is necessary if a good gunmount is to result.

The first thing to do is carefully mount the gun so that the muzzles are pointing just above the point from behind which the target will first appear. Then, as the target comes, over the hedge, the gun will be found to be pointing behind it. This is intended.

When the target appears, the number one priority is for the eyes to be focused on it to the exclusion of all else. It is not good enough just to *look* at the target. This requires intense visual concentration and beginners find it very difficult at first—it is most tempting to have a quick peek at the barrels to 'make sure they are lined up'. However, this is about as effective as looking at a cricket bat as you attempt to hit the ball!

All movements follow from correct focusing on the target and its importance cannot be overstressed.

So, having got the target clearly focused, the muzzles are swung from behind the target, up to it and past it, the shot being fired as, or just after, the gun passes the target.

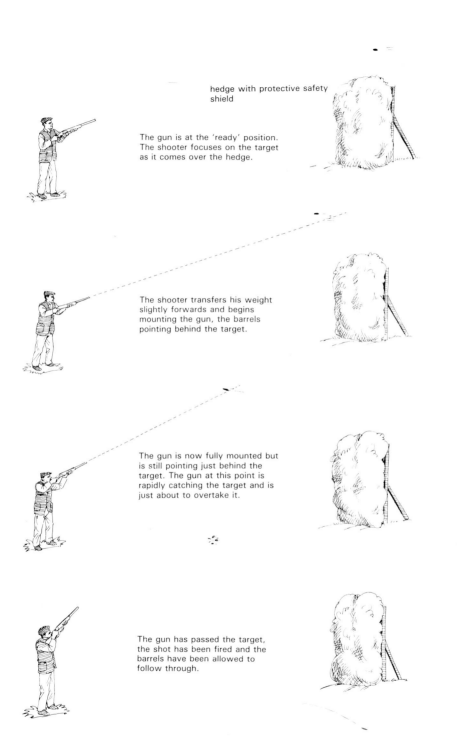

hedge with protective safety shield

The gun is at the 'ready' position. The shooter focuses on the target as it comes over the hedge.

The shooter transfers his weight slightly forwards and begins mounting the gun, the barrels pointing behind the target.

The gun is now fully mounted but is still pointing just behind the target. The gun at this point is rapidly catching the target and is just about to overtake it.

The gun has passed the target, the shot has been fired and the barrels have been allowed to follow through.

Gun/target relationship when shooting at a straight incoming target.

To achieve this, all that is necessary is for the left hand to push the barrels upwards. Notice that the gun's position in the shoulder and against the face must not change at all as the muzzles are being pushed up. At no time must the gun be allowed to move independently of the upper body *regardless of the angle or height of the shot.*

This shooter displays good arching of the back. Note the weight remains on the forward foot even when the target is high overhead.

It will also be seen from the illustration that the weight remains over the forward foot for this particular shot and that the body arches back slightly to enable the gun to be swung to the target without restriction. At some point during the swing the shot must be fired, but when? It is something which varies from person to person, whatever the textbooks might say, and there can be no hard and fast rules applied. This I must try to explain.

During the time it takes for the shot charge to leave the barrel and reach the target, the target will have moved on, the distance it will have moved being determined by the velocity of the shot charge, the range of the target, and its speed. To compensate for this movement, at the moment of firing the barrels must be pointing sufficiently ahead of the target so that the shot charge and the target will meet on a collision course. This holds true on every target, other than those flying with no apparent deviation either directly away or directly towards the shooter, and these are rarely encountered. Most targets are rising or dropping, as well as moving left or right, however slightly.

The problem lies with how different shooters see this forward allowance, or lead as it is known. The eyes, remember, are focused on the target and must never be allowed to flick out ahead of it to check that the lead is correct. So how is lead observed? The answer is that it is not observed. It is felt or sensed but never actually measured off in the calculated way that a rifle shooter would do it.

For some shooters, the *feel* of each and every shot, regardless of range, speed or angle, is that they have swung the gun from behind the target and that they have pulled the trigger at the precise moment the target has been passed by the muzzles. Whatever lead happens to be necessary, and there must be some, occurs for them automatically, with no conscious effort involved at all.

At the other end of the scale are those shooters who are quite aware of and feel every bit of lead required to hit any target. Such lead will not be registered in feet and inches because this would make the whole thing impossible. Nevertheless, these shooters have to *feel* that they have allowed the gun to pass the target by the required amount before firing. They will *feel* to be slightly ahead of shallow-angled close targets, further ahead of wider targets, and considerably ahead of the long-range targets.

In between these two examples are the majority who, while not feeling that they give big leads to long-range targets, nevertheless do not feel that they can shoot almost right at their targets, either.

At this point follow-through must be mentioned. If the shot is to be successful, it is essential that the gun continues moving *after* the shot has been fired. The movement need not be exaggerated, but the target should be seen to be well broken (or missed) before the swing is allowed to slow and stop. Certainly, the gun must not stop as the shot is fired.

Meanwhile, back to the target which has just come over the hedge. When to fire at it? Initially, the shooter is advised to fire as the gun is *passing* the target, making sure that there is no slowing of the gun's movement as the trigger is pulled.

The sequence, then, is to focus the eyes on the target, move the muzzles smoothly up from behind the target and overtake it, then fire as it is passed, being careful not to allow the swing to slow or stop. On this example target, if everything is done correctly, very little lead is required and after a few shots targets should start to break.

Once this is working fairly well (don't expect to hit them all yet!)

the shooter can move onto the next stage. It entails starting with the gun in the 'ready' position rather than in the shoulder and at first this is a bit more difficult, though the stance is just the same as before.

As with all shots, the most important thing is to get the target in focus the moment it appears. The next action is to allow the weight to transfer more on to the forward foot. It will make the whole shot more balanced and controllable. The gun is then pushed forward towards the target, the two hands working in unison. The earlier action

Weight transference to the forward foot improves balance and control.

of initially pointing the gun behind the target is repeated here, the only difference being that the muzzles must be made to catch the target *as* the gun is being mounted, *not* after. Ideally, the gun will reach the fully mounted position fractionally before the target is caught by the muzzles.

The vast majority of beginners (and quite a few more seasoned shooters) make the mistake of first raising the butt of the gun to the shoulder, which leaves the barrels pointing at the ground. This means the muzzles are pointing considerably behind the target, something which can only be corrected by making a fast, barrel-only swing with the gun. This in turn means that the gun must move independently of the rest of the body and this does not work too well! Possibly the best image that a beginner can have in his mind at the commencement of the swing is of the muzzles being pointed with the left hand towards the approaching target at the same time as the right hand raises the stock smoothly to the shoulder.

The stock must not be allowed to drift away from the body during this mounting movement. It must slide lightly up the side of the chest until, at the instant the stock comes to the face, the shoulder is hunched forward to meet it. The gun *is not* pulled back to the shoulder.

Notice that any abrupt raising of the stock will make the muzzles dip. The left hand has further to travel during most shots and therefore care must be exercised to see that it is not allowed to trail behind the movement of the right hand.

As with all sports, the presence of an experienced person is very useful during this initial outing. He can check basic gunmounting and swing as well as marking where the shots are going when the targets are missed. Better still, of course, is to have the services of a competent instructor.

**The master eye**
It is during these first few shots that the shooter can be checked to see which of his eyes is the master. With both eyes open and a gun which fits tolerably well the shots should all go straight, even if some are inevitably behind or in front of the target. Many ladies, most children and quite a few men will find that with both eyes open they shoot somewhat to the left. The whys and wherefores of this are discussed in Gun Fit (page 39).

One point must be mentioned, though. Some shooters insist that to shoot well it is necessary to shoot with both eyes open, regardless of whether one shoots straight or not. The inference is that an eye problem is something which can be corrected with practice—it cannot.

If, for whatever reason a shooter has to close an eye, then close an eye he must. However, any shooter who has to shoot with an eye closed need not feel that he is doomed to a lifetime of inferior shooting. That would be a very dismal prospect. However, there is no point in denying that shooting with two eyes open has a number of advantages: depth perception, quality of vision, ability to focus easily on the target; all these things and more are sacrificed or reduced when shooting with an eye shut.

Having said that, before giving the whole thing up, bear in mind that there are European, World, and Olympic champions who have shot and regularly won whilst shooting with just one eye!

## The left crossing target

The principle for this target is exactly the same as that of the incomer, and we are assuming once again that it is coming from behind the hedge but this time going left instead of straight.

The muzzles must again be started behind the target and on its flight line, the gun being mounted *as* the target is being caught. As with any other shot, to mount the gun and then swing is wrong, and once more the hands must work together on this. If the stock is mounted abruptly, the muzzles will dip below the flight line and the shot will go under the target. Correct use of the left hand is the secret.

The weight must remain on the left foot throughout this shot, while the right foot pivots as in a golf swing. It will have several benefits. Balance will be maintained, the swing will be free-moving, and the shoulders will be able to turn square to the target.

As can be seen from the photograph, the swing entails a complete turn of the upper body during which the shoulders must remain square to the *line of flight* of the target. This last point is very important. Should the left shoulder dip instead of turn, then the gun will be dragged down from the flightline of the target, causing a miss below.

The sequence then is as follows. The target appears, going to the left. The shooter focuses his gaze on it, and with the muzzles pointing just behind the target, he begins to swing and mount the gun in one co-ordinated movement. The gun should come into the fully mounted position just before the muzzles reach the target. The swing continues so that the muzzles catch and pass the target. When the target has been passed, the shot is fired. Throughout this sequence the eyes are fixed on the target.

Forward allowance? As with the straight target, initially try shooting just as the gun is passing the target. *Actual* measurable lead on a target like this, i.e. a target going relatively slowly, not too wide and about fifteen yeards away, is about two feet. How *you personally* see it is something with which you will have to experiment.

## The right crossing target

In principle this is the same as the left crosser but there are a few differences brought about by the fact that the gun sits in the right shoulder. This tends to make the swing to the right a little more awkward and for beginners it can cause an annoying number of shots to miss behind the target.

Generally speaking, the weight should be again on the left foot but for some shooters this will make turning to the right physically quite difficult. For these people the weight can be allowed to transfer to the right foot so that the left foot pivots—the exact opposite to the movement recommended for the left target, in fact.

However, while this makes the swing to the right slightly easier, it can also cause instability if care is not exercised. Also, when two targets flying in opposite directions are encountered, the weight change from one foot to the other between shots can produce much swaying about. If it works best for you, though, use it.

The approach to this target is the same as for the incomer and the one going to the left. The muzzles start behind, the gun is swung through the target and the shot is fired.

As mentioned earlier, most beginners will regularly shoot behind the target. To overcome the problem, a good idea is to feel that the shot is being fired further ahead of the target than seems normal, that is, having shot the left target and experienced the feel of the forward allowance, give this one a bit more. It does not sound very scientific, but it works.

Must the eyes be allowed to look ahead of the target to encourage this extra lead? No! As previously emphasised, the eyes must focus *on the target*, nowhere else. The shooter must just *feel* that the muzzles are pointing more ahead, that's all.

Finally, a good follow-through is essential if this shot is to work at all.

## Doubles

Firing two shots in quick succession, whether at a single target or at two, will be examined more closely in the various chapters on specific disciplines.

For the beginner, he will have his work cut out just learning how to deal with one shot and one target at a time!

# 6

# Sporting Clays

Of all the forms of clay target shooting practised throughout the world, Sporting comes closest to simulating actual shots which might be encountered by the game shooter when he is in the field. Consequently, since no two Sporting layouts are ever exactly the same, this form of clay shooting is as far removed from the idea of a discipline as it is possible to be. Let me hasten to add that such a statement is not meant as an insult to Sporting clay shooting, far from it! This form of shooting is almost certainly responsible for at least 90% of all those who shoot clays in Great Britain starting in the first place, mostly at some small local Sporting shoot. At the other end of the scale Sporting, as shot under the rules of FITASC, is arguably the most demanding form of clay shooting in existence.

Because of the very variable nature of the targets from shoot to shoot, performance valuation from achieved scores is not really valid, although it is the only means available to the CPSA for the establishment of classification. Unfortunately, owing to the variations in shoot difficulty, a score of 80 ex 100 might only just scrape into the first ten in one competition, whereas at another it might well run away with the first prize.

Averages, then, mean less at Sporting than they do at Skeet or Trap; the object, as in game shooting, is to shoot as many of the targets as are presented.

## English Sporting

This is undoubtedly the most popular form of clay shooting in Great Britain and it is easy to understand why. Setting up a small Sporting clay shoot requires none of the financial outlay unavoidable in Trap or Skeet, and only a relatively small piece of land is needed. With understanding neighbours it is possible to hold a Sporting shoot on as little as one acre, although that is probably a minimum. When I first started clay shooting we used to shoot at a place with hardly more ground than this and yet they managed to squeeze in four separate stands without actually endangering life, and even held an annual competition for all comers. It was a gentle introduction to clay shooting and one I would recommend to anyone contemplating joining the ranks.

Most of these small clubs shoot twice a month, the maximum permitted by law without recourse to planning permission. Such permission, if sought, is seldom granted since many of these small clubs are within hearing distance of dwelling places, the inhabitants of which are understandably reluctant to be blown out of their beds on a Sunday morning by nearby shotgun shooting! In spite of this it is a sure bet that in any fairly rural area there will be one or more such clubs not too far away from anyone wishing to join.

The various national clay shooting associations in Great Britain can locate your nearest small club for you although unfortunately at the present time many of these remain unaffiliated. The only way to find them is by local knowledge, and here pubs are often good sources of information. The other way, when a local club is known to exist but cannot be located, is to drive around the area with the car windows open. Many otherwise hidden clubs may be detected by sound.

At most of the better clubs there are various officials whose job it is to make the use of the club facilities safe and enjoyable for the members and their guests. The safety officer is undoubtedly the most important of these, being in charge of the siting of the clay throwers (traps) as well as the establishment of safe paths between the various stands. It is also his task to ensure that everyone behaves in a safe and responsible fashion, and that correct gun handling is strictly observed. Offenders will receive a stern warning for minor infringements and will quite rightly get their marching orders for anything more serious. Where firearms are concerned unsafe behaviour or horseplay cannot be tolerated.

Another important figure is the club coach who will have attended and passed (we hope!) the CPSA coaching course. He will be responsible for introducing the beginners to clay shooting at the same time as instilling in them essential safety procedures. Being perfectly safe with the gun (as well as being seen to be safe) is far more important than mere proficiency at breaking clay targets.

Fortunately, clay shooters pride themselves on their excellent safety record and rightly so. When one is conditioned by clay shooting to expect 100% safety consciousness from one's fellow shooters, it comes as an unpleasant shock to encounter supposedly intelligent men behaving in a dangerous fashion when game shooting. Here, all too frequently, closed and loaded guns are waved about indiscriminately whilst waiting for the beaters to get in position, the gun being held in the crook of the arm and pointing at everyone else's feet. Happily, such things do not happen at clay shoots.

By their very nature, these smaller clubs present targets which can be shot by anyone reasonably competent, and for many Sunday morning shooters that is enough. For those aspiring to greater things it is probably necessary to look farther afield. There are quite a number of more permanent shooting grounds about with correspondingly more sophisticated layouts, and they will have such things as towers capable of presenting high targets at a variety of angles and certainly they will have a greater selection of shooting stands, too. The targets at such places are likely to be a good deal more testing than those thrown by the smaller clubs and because of this they are, to the more experienced and better shooter, more interesting.

For competitions on a grand scale the shooting schools or large clubs come into their own, and it is at these that the very high towers are encountered, often throwing targets a hundred feet high or more. A perfect example of this is the high tower at the West London Shooting Grounds, Northolt, regularly the venue for the annual British Sporting Championships. The tower is about 120 ft high and the crossing targets from it look very small indeed. Theoretically, they *can* be broken with a .410 but most people, in truth, struggle to hit them with a 12-bore.

## Sporting targets

Unlike those encountered on the Skeet field, Sporting targets cannot be so readily categorised. Such evocative stand titles as 'Diving Duck' and 'Rocketing Pheasants' can be interpreted in a variety of ways, all of which are entirely at the whim of the shoot organisers. Target difficulty is largely dependent (or ought to be) on the quality of the competitors likely to participate.

For instance, at something like the British Sporting Championships the organisers will be attempting to set the targets in such a way that the 'High Gun' will break something in the region of 88-92 ex 100, with the winner of 'C' class shooting around 70-74.

Believe me, setting a course like this is no easy task. No one will thank the organisers if the High Gun struggles to shoot 80 ex 100 because lower down the field the rest of the competitors will have had a miserable time. On the other hand, a very high-scoring shoot is going to bore all but the novices.

To achieve the necessary balance, most shoots are set up with a percentage of relatively easy stands on which the average shot will expect to get six or seven out of the ten, whilst the top shooter will be looking to hit all of them. Other stands will be more difficult, with two or three of them requiring very fine shooting in order to break six or seven targets.

One of the features of English Sporting is that virtually all the stands will involve the shooting of doubles, either released together or 'on report'. For those unfamiliar with Sporting, the latter expression refers to the type of double where the second target is released only when the first has been shot at. This by no means infers that this particular type of double is easy! More often than not it is comprised of two targets which, if thrown simultaneously, would be impossible. A typical example of this is often found on the 'Driven Grouse' stand where the first target is an incomer, usually low and very fast, while the second target is a low one, zipping away from behind and to the side of the shooter; not too difficult for the best shots maybe, but certainly not easy.

More testing is the sort of thing frequently thrown from the high towers: a straight over target is followed, on report, by a wide target crossing to the shooter's left. The next double again has the first target straight over, but the second this time goes wide to the right. After the four target sequence has been repeated three times it is a very good shot indeed (or a very lucky one!) who comes away from the stand having missed none of them.

While there is no denying that nothing can ever really substitute for basic talent, there are easy and not so easy ways to tackle all the targets thrown in a Sporting clay competition. Knowing the easy ways is a big step towards improving scores and the following should help the struggling sporting shooter gain those very desirable extra few targets.

## Towards consistency

The shooter striving to improve his scores must try to eliminate as many variables from his style as possible, because it is these which result in inconsistent performance.

Without doubt, regular training in gunmount and swing can only be beneficial provided it is done intelligently (see Training Methods on page 133). The intention must be to develop a method which, rather like a good golfer's swing, repeats itself exactly for each and every shot.

This may seem a tall order and it is, but nothing worth achieving ever comes easily; for the shooter who masters it, the biggest variables of all—the targets themselves—can be handled with a good deal more confidence and expectation of success.

The Churchill 'ready' position.

## Gun ready position

Possibly the best 'ready' position for both game and Sporting clay shooting is that recommended some years ago by the late Robert Churchill who, among his many claims to fame, was a notable shooting instructor. His stock-tucked-into-the-armpit position has the following benefits:

1  Regardless of the shot being taken, the movement of gun to shoulder is always the same. Starting with the gun in a variety of different positions can lead to inconsistent gunmounting and missed targets.
2  With the gun tucked into the armpit it is practically impossible to lift the stock abruptly into the shoulder, leaving the muzzles pointing at the ground instead of the target. (This is very common and one of the movements most destructive to good shooting.)
3  It encourages the correct use of the leading hand, i.e. to point the muzzles towards the target, a very positive movement.

The vital initial move of 3 is evident in the performance of *every* top shooter (watch them and see), whereas the bad move of 2 is frequently to be seen whenever a poor or below average shot is in action.

The actual place to where the gun points when in this correct ready position is controlled by the height and direction of the target to be shot. In taking a straight incoming target as an example, the muzzles must never be allowed to point at a spot lower than that from which the target will appear. (This is as the shooter sees the muzzles; they will actually be pointing rather higher.)

The shooter aligns the muzzle (as he sees it) just above the position where he will first detect the target.

Diagram showing muzzle height relative to target exit point.

If the target is appearing from behind a hedge then the muzzles should be directed to the top of the hedge; if it is coming off the top of a tower, that is the place to point the muzzles. A common mistake is to allow the muzzles to droop so low that they are pointing at the ground, thus almost guaranteeing that the shooter has little chance of making a controlled swing at the target when it appears. The usual result of starting in such a position is that the shooter has to resort to a wild sweep, hardly the recipe for success!

A similar rule needs to be applied when tackling crossing targets. The ready position on these shots should be such that the muzzles are pointing on the anticipated flightline of the target, never well above or below. Where the muzzles point relative to the starting point of the target is dependent on the nature of the target concerned. If the target presents the shooter with a fairly leisurely shot with plenty of time available in which to get the gun moving, then the muzzles can happily be pointed right at the trap. If, on the other hand (and far more likely!), the target is fast and allows little time in which to shoot, then the gun can be pointed out from the trap. In other words, on a target going to the shooter's left the muzzles should be pointed to the left of the target's starting place.

With a fast crossing target it is usually better not to point the gun right at the trap. Here, with a right-to-left crossing target, the shooter looks towards 'A' (the trap) while the gun is pointed towards 'B'.

Address position for fast targets: example shows the position for a target flying from right to left.

## Stance

Unlike Skeet, Sporting does not seem to have become afflicted with weird and wonderful styles, many of which tend to hinder rather than help performance. This is possibly due to the fact that many Sporting clay shooters are also game or pigeon shots, where to stand all day in a contorted position would soon prove to be not only uncomfortable but also unproductive.

Whatever type of clay shooting one practises there can be little doubt that you cannot beat a perfectly natural stance and posture. This means standing in a relaxed way, with the trunk more or less erect and the feet no more than shoulder-width apart, preferably less. From this neutral position it is then possible to move freely in any direction without losing balance or control of the gun. Actual foot position within the stance tends to vary according to the shot, so more of that later.

None of the foregoing is new; all good shots do these things automatically, although many of them are probably unaware of the fact. This is particularly true of those who have shot all their lives. They simply look at the target, swing and shoot. Their action is instinctive.

The late starter, and this in my opinion is anyone who begins shooting in their twenties or after, is less fortunate. He or she must learn to shoot 'by numbers', but with a dedicated approach and attention to detail there is no reason why the late beginner should not eventually shoot just as well as the so-called naturals.

## Observation

One of the most useful aspects of the learning process is that of careful observation. English Sporting is unique among the various types of clay shooting in that it is possible to get very close to the people actually shooting without distracting them. The only time a Trap or Skeet shooter gets near another competitor in this way is when he, too, is shooting and this is no time to watch other people. The Sporting shot, on the other hand, has plenty of time to wander around from stand to stand and watch some of the action before he himself is involved.

This is an excellent opportunity for the person wishing to improve to move close to the really good shots and watch them at work. By this I mean watch *them*, not the targets at which they are shooting. Ignore any mannerisms and try to absorb the sense of rhythm, which is so important to good shooting, and the smooth, economical movement. Observe how the targets, while not rushed, are nevertheless taken quickly and efficiently.

It is amazing how often some of the magic can rub off on the observer. It is worthwhile actually basing your style on that of someone you may particularly admire, just as a young cricketer often models his action on that of a county player.

# Sporting stands

As has already been said, the variations on the Sporting target theme are legion; no two stands are ever quite the same and, of course, Sporting shooters would have it no other way. However, because of this it is only possible to generalise about particular Sporting-type shots, there being no specifics from which to work.

The following, therefore, is in no way comprehensive nor could it be, though most stands encountered by the Sporting shooter will fall within one or other of the examples.

## The 'driven' targets

As mentioned earlier in the chapter, certain stands at any Sporting shoot are on the easy side and most of the better shots will be looking to get the lot when shooting them. Excluding the high tower targets, which are unlikely to be considered easy by even the most accomplished shooters, these stands will usually feature the 'driven' type of target, so-called because they represent the type of bird likely to be encountered by a game shooter when out on a day's driven pheasants or partridges, etc.

In their simplest form they will be a pair of targets released simultaneously and flying either straight over the shooter or, more likely, to his left or right. If it is the intention of the organisers that this be a high scoring stand then the targets will rarely be more than forty feet high, although they may still be quite quick. (They are not intended to be too easy.)

The first thing to decide about these targets is which one to take first and, often enough, this is something which will not take much figuring out. For instance, if one target is flying straight over the shooter while the other is going to his left or right, the straight target is *always* the one to take first and it is easy enough to understand why. The low straight target is a simple shot, providing it is taken out in front of the shooter and not right above his head. Taken this late it becomes a very tricky proposition; taken second in the double that is just what it will become!

To take the first straight target the shooter has to set himself up as described earlier; the gun is pointed at or slightly above the place from which the target will first appear and the targets are called for. When the pair appears it is essential that the crossing target is initially ignored, since you cannot focus on two at the same time. Trying to do so will possibly result in both being missed.

The very first move, and one which with practice soon becomes automatic, is a slight transference of weight onto the leading foot. Attempting to shoot this target by throwing the weight backwards tends to take the control of the gun away from the hands and arms, and usually means that the shooter becomes so unbalanced that getting to the second target is very difficult, if not impossible.

At the same time as the weight is being eased onto the forward foot the leading hand must begin pushing the muzzles towards the target.

Essential here is that the muzzles must be pointing just *behind* the target, not in front of it.

The job of the rear hand is to bring the gun smoothly to the shoulder. This must be co-ordinated with what the leading hand is doing, of course, and must never be allowed to dominate the action. Should it do so the muzzles will inevitably dip, leaving them pointing a long way behind the target. Ideally, the muzzles will be gradually catching the target as the gun is being mounted, thus setting in motion the swing which will bring the muzzles onto and past the target in the approved fashion.

The actual track which the muzzles follow must be exactly that being flown by the target. A poor gunmount, particularly if the stock is away from the cheek instead of on it, will take the muzzles out of this track and the shot will go to the side of the target. (For a right-handed shooter the shot will almost certainly go to the left and *vice versa*.)

As this swing progresses, taking the gun muzzles up to and through the target, the body should arch backwards with the weight remaining over the leading foot, the leg of which should be straight though not stiff. This arching of the body, with the weight still forward, allows the shooter to swing freely without fear of falling backwards.

The full gunmount should be completed just before the muzzles reach the target and without checking the smooth motion of the swing when they have passed it. How far ahead of the target the gun is pointing when the trigger is pulled depends to a great extent on how the shooter sees lead and, of course, how high and fast the target happens to be. (See Basic Technique on page 51.)

Most important of all is that the eyes remain sharply focused on the target until the shot has been fired. A very common and fatal error is to start looking for the second target before the first has been shot, so if trouble is being experienced on the first targets of any doubles make sure this is not the cause.

All the foregoing takes much less time to do than to read, of course, and it must be co-ordinated into one smooth movement if it is to be successful.

Having got the first target shot, attention must immediately be switched to the second which will by now be heading somewhere off to the side. We'll assume for the moment that in this particular instance it is not flying at a wide angle to the shooter.

As the second target is being located by the eyes the stock must be dropped out of the shoulder, although the amount it drops must never be lower than that of the 'ready' position, and with the target clearly focused the muzzles are placed behind the target and on its flightline.

The swing is similar to the one used to take the first target. With the weight still on the forward foot the gun is swung through the target, the gunmount occurring, as with the straight target, just before the target is caught.

The movement of the body is important here. It is essentially a turn which is centred on the leading leg and must never be allowed to degenerate into a twisting motion. Such twisting causes the shoulder to drop and so throws the gun off line. Throughout this turning movement, the shoulders must remain square to the target.

Having swung through the target the shot is fired, the amount of lead required depending once again on the target and the shooter. However, for the sort of target described here, no more than twenty to twenty-five yards away, it is probable that the lead would be two to three feet. Remember though, this measurement means very little. It is how you, the shooter, see it that matters and this is something you have to find out for yourself.

As with all shots, do not forget the importance of a good follow-through even on the first target of a double. When pushed to shoot quickly at fast targets the gun must still be moving after the shot has been fired or the target will almost certainly be missed.

When the second target is flying at a wider angle than the one described it will be necessary to swing as before, but this time the weight will be transferred fully to the leading foot. In addition, there will be a distinct leaning in of the body towards the target, and this is particularly true if the target is low. As with the closer crossing target, however, it is essential that this is still a turning motion and not a tilt of the shoulders.

Many newcomers to shooting become confused when hearing the varying ideas regarding the amount of forward allowance required in order to hit a given target. It is particularly difficult when shooter A, a well-known and very competent performer, says that the target needs a lead of two feet, whereas shooter B, equally famous, says it needs six feet.

Who is right? The answer, unfortunately, is that they both are! They are both describing what they individually *see* when they shoot the target. What the *real* lead happens to be is irrelevant to them—it is how they personally see it that matters, nothing else.

The newcomer, upon reading this, will possibly feel somewhat despairing but in a surprisingly short time he will soon discover his own 'lead pictures'. The only way to do so is to shoot!

**Pair to the left or right**
Deciding which target to take first, when both are heading in the same direction, is straightforward enough: always take the closer one. With most stands being surrounded by safety cages there is a limit as to how far the gun may be swung in any direction, and a little thought soon reveals that the narrower the angle of the target, the quicker it reaches and goes beyond that limit.

The principle involved in taking these targets is exactly the same as for the two just described. The first target is swung through from behind and shot, the gun is lowered from the shoulder so that the muzzles are on line with and behind the second target, then this in its turn is swung through and the shot fired.

The only modification, and one not used by all the top shooters, is to the 'ready' position. In order to make the swing slightly more free-moving, many shooters like to stand in such a way that they are favouring the direction in which the pair of targets will be flying. On a pair flying to the left, for instance, the shooter will stand in a position facing a point possibly mid-way between the clay trap and the limits of the safety cage. Having done this, he then turns back to his correct starting position which will be either with the gun pointing at the trap stand or slightly to the left of it. Set up this way he is then able to tackle the targets with a swing already 'pre-programmed'.

Whether this adjustment suits you or not is a matter for experiment. Whatever you do, though, do not get coiled up like a spring, for this tends to take away the all-important control from the hands and arms.

**The high tower**
The nemesis of many otherwise competent shooters, the high tower is usually one of the 'feature' stands at any big shoot, with prizes often given for anyone who manages to shoot the lot.

One of the main problems with such targets is their extreme range and the fact that usually there is more than enough time in which to shoot them. This latter fact would seem to be a plus to the layman, but anyone who has shot pheasants knows only too well that the bird most often missed is the one that comes from a long way off. Shotgun shooting is an art very reliant on conditioned reflexes and most experienced shots prefer something that comes at them fast and unexpectedly. The slip fielder in cricket will react and catch a ball that he hardly even sees, whereas standing further back, that same man can drop a seemingly easy lob that falls right into his hands. Why? Because, as with the high tower shots, there is too much time in which to think. The conscious mind, acting more slowly, takes over what should be an entirely unconscious and instinctive action. It is only too easy on these high targets to start calculating lead and taking deliberate aim down the rib, seeking to make certain. Unfortunately, the only certainty is that the target will be missed.

The basic technique is much the same as for the previous targets, although on any of these high targets the stance should be somewhat narrower than usual. The swing is going to be longer, and the narrow stance will permit this without the swing getting bound up. Many of the best high target shooters stand with their feet almost together, and it is well worth experimenting with. Try to stand with the feet as close together as possible, consistent with maintaining good balance.

How the body weight should be distributed is somewhat dependent on the shooter's physical make-up. Fairly slim people are able to shoot targets at a point well past the vertical, with their weight planted firmly on the front foot and the rear heel eased off the ground for good balance. This entails the arching back of the body as described earlier. Those of stocky build, or even the rotund, can often benefit from a back-foot stance, but care must be exercised since this still involves a degree of back arching.

Percy Stanbury, one of the great names in the shooting world and a fine shooting instructor, is notably tall and slim and he advocates the former stance. The late Robert Churchill, equally famous in his time, was short and stocky and he, of course, plumped for the latter. Churchill was also a great believer in standing on the left foot for left-crossing targets and on the right foot for those going the other way. Stanbury believes that all shots should be taken with the weight on the left foot. Again, I think this comes down to personal build, and suggest that you be guided by your reflection in the mirror.

Once the stance has been decided, the next decision to make is where to point the gun when in the ready position. For straight over targets the best place is right at the top of the tower, no lower, with the gun tucked comfortably, but not too tightly, into the armpit.

When the target appears it will look rather small but, nevertheless, the eyes must focus on it immediately. With the gun dancing about inches from the eyes it is all too easy to look at this instead of that little aspirin up there, but don't let it happen.

With the eyes glued to the target the gun is brought smoothly up from behind it, mounted and swung through, all in one flowing movement. Ensure that the hands do not get out of synchronisation during this swing. During any swing the leading hand has much further to travel than the rear one and on the high target it is important that the leading hand, while not totally dominating the swing, must always be in charge of pointing the muzzles to the target. Any rear hand domination, i.e. an abrupt mounting of the stock to the face, will cause the barrels to point very low and if this happens on these high tower shots, there is little hope of recovering the lost ground between muzzles and target.

Where possible, the straight over target should be taken just before the vertical. Taken here, it is at its nearest point to the shooter (important at such long range) while still being reasonably easy from a freedom-of-swing point of view.

It is quite possible to hit a target that has gone beyond this point, safety cage permitting, but remember that wherever the target happens to be in the sky, the gun must go some way beyond it to get the necessary forward allowance. Unless you are particularly flexible, try to take it earlier whenever possible.

During this swinging-through movement, the barrels will inevitably come between the shooter's master eye and the target, and this is a very critical point in the shot. Whatever happens, the eyes must not be drawn to the gun. For the person who shoots both eyes open, it is not too much of a problem. If he really concentrates his full attention on the target, he will still see it even though the barrels have blotted out the view of the master eye. This is because the other eye will still see the target and, in the short time interval between passing the target and pulling the trigger, the fact that the master eye is 'blind' will make no difference to the outcome of the shot.

For the person who for one reason or another shoots with an eye closed the problem may well seem insurmountable. However, if the eye is focused properly on the target and this focus is held *after* the target is passed, then the shot will come off just as if the eye were still actually seeing the target perfectly. In effect, the eye continues to register the target's position in the sky even though it cannot see it, but this only works as long as the brain is fooled into thinking that the eye still *can* see!

Forward allowance, in *real* terms, can be quite considerable on these high targets but once again it is what the shooter himself sees that really matters. Some people may be heard to say 'You've got to give that one a five bar gate!', meaning they see a lot of forward allowance when they shoot. Others, equally successful, will probably shake their heads in disagreement and claim that they shoot right at it.

Once again, even on targets as high and as far away as these, opinions as to the forward allowance required vary between several yards and none. The only answer is to try it, for only by experience will you arrive at your personal solution. You will very soon discover whether or not you need to see lead when you shoot, as it will become immediately apparent on even the relatively close-range targets. It is important to avoid slavishly following someone else's casual opinion on this particular subject because, unlike most other aspects of shotgun shooting, two totally opposite ideas can both be right. Nevertheless, be guided by your coach.

**High double**

One of the great truths in shotgun shooting is the seemingly foolish and therefore frequently ignored observation that 'You can't hit two targets if you miss the first one!' While this may seem a blatant case of overstating the obvious it is, in fact, rather more subtle than it first appears. What it means is that if you concern yourself too much with what the second target is doing you can easily make the mistake of forgetting about the first one and you will probably miss it. This can lead to a situation where the shooter is not only thinking about the second target while shooting at the first, but he is actually looking at it, too!

This can often happen when shooting at any long-range targets which are flying relatively close together. Because they are only a few yards apart and at such a range, the eyes need hardly move to switch from one to the other, or even worse, look at both at once.

There are many tricks advised by game shooters to avoid this sort of thing. They often find themselves confronted by coveys of grouse or partridge, which may easily number fifty or more, flying almost wing tip to wing tip. It might be thought by the layman that a quick shot in amongst the general group would knock down half-a-dozen or more, 'browning' the covey as it is known by initiates. Strangely enough, this very rarely happens. Shots fired in such a way must lack conviction, I suppose, but whatever the reason they rarely succeed. What the wise game shooter does is to pick his bird from the pack and concentrate on its head or maybe even its beak—anything to ensure that the eyes are rivetted to the bird and nothing else.

The clay shooter does not have any heads or beaks to look at but he does have a front: the front edge of the clay target. If you are prone to looking away from the first target of long-range pairs before the shot is fired, try to concentrate on the front edge. (Theoretically, any edge would do but looking at the back edge of *any* target, let alone a long-range one, is asking for the shot to go behind.)

The technique required for a high double is the same as for any other pair of targets. If the pair is flying straight over, it does not really matter which of them you take first. There will be a considerable follow-through on the first target you shoot, and this means that the gun will be pointing well ahead of the second target and to the side of it. To correct this, the gun is eased out of the shoulder and the muzzles dropped down to a point directly behind the second target. Notice that the gun must leave the shoulder, even though only slightly, so that you can start a whole new swing for this one. If you try just to take the mounted gun straight across the the second target, you will invariably miss it.

This re-setting of the gun for the second targets of doubles is something that must occur regardless of the nature of the targets. On

Shooter taking a double from the high tower.

some, such as very close grouse-type shots, where the targets are invariably low and fast, this easing between shots may only be a slight relaxing of muscle tension, with hardly any movement from the shoulder at all. On no simultaneous double does the gun ever come right down to the 'ready' position. In the case of our high straight over double the muzzles must be dropped sufficiently to place them behind the second target, but the actual movement of the stock from the shoulder need only be an inch or so, no more.

At the completion of the second shot the shooter should still be poised in a well-balanced position, not falling over backwards. Initially, the 'arching back' movement may be a little stiff, but a lot of dry practice helps to learn this balanced movement and, once acquired, it will make a substantial difference to high target shooting.

**Doubles high and wide**
If the shoot organisers want to keep the high tower as a low-scoring stand, all they have to do is throw simultaneous targets in opposite directions! If they are only slightly to the left and right, then they can be taken as though they were straight over targets, but if they are wider than this, watch out. If one is fairly straight and the other wide, it is not so bad and the obvious one to tackle first is the straighter of the two.

As mentioned earlier, some shooters like to stand round a while to favour the second target, turning themselves back to the tower for the first straight one. This is something with which the individual shooter can experiment.

If the second target is flying 'against the gun' then it is almost certainly better to stand round in this way. (This means a target flying to the right of a right-handed shooter and *vice versa*.) Whichever way the shooter stands, for the second wide target the stock should be dropped further from the shoulder than was necessary on the previous example, as this will make it easier to get the muzzles correctly positioned behind the second target and on its flightline.

It is this second target that causes most people trouble, and not just because it is often a very long shot. A common error, which all of us make on these high and wide targets, is that of dropping the shoulder instead of turning squarely. On a left target, for instance, the left shoulder drops and when this happens it becomes increasingly difficult to keep the gun up on the target's flightline. It is then quite likely that the shot will go underneath. Turn properly and then not only is the swing so much easier, it also encourages the muzzles to stay up on line.

At the sort of height we are talking about, a simultaneous double, with the targets heading wide in opposite directions, is about as difficult a pair of targets as the Sporting shooter is likely to encounter, 'silly' ones excepted. (More about these later.)

Sorting out which to take first is number one priority on these two targets. There are four possibilities.

1 Take the one which you feel most confident about and then do your best on the second.

2 Take the one you feel least confident about first while you have sufficient time to shoot it and still get to your favourite.

3 Take the target which is most awkward to shoot first in terms of freedom of swing. This will be the right-crossing target for right-handed shooters, and *vice versa*.

4 Do the opposite of 3.

The top shooters, who will want to hit them all, will almost certainly do 3. The target going wide and left of the left-handed shooter, for instance, will be very difficult for him if he takes it second in the double, since any swing in this direction tends to get progressively more restricted the further he has to go. By taking this one first, he is able to swing quite freely at the second target flying to his left, as far as the limitations imposed by the safety cage allow.

Some top shooters prefer the shot 'against the gun', however, and they may well do 4, although this is not recommended for the average performer. For them 1 must be the best option, since it is undeniably more satisfactory to hit one target than miss two!

Between shots the gun must come right down almost to the familiar 'ready' position and from here picking up the second wide target is considerably easier than it would be if the gun were to be just 'eased' from the shoulder. It is also very important that the muzzles are taken smoothly to a point no more than a few yards behind the second target before the re-mount begins. Re-mounting the gun much sooner than this will make the swing very long and slow, with the muzzles 'out of touch' with the target.

By now the second target will be well on its way to the outfield and without doubt it will require, in *actual* terms, a pretty big lead. As we know, this all depends on how the individual sees it, of course. Sufficient to say that any tendency towards aiming down the rib will *not* succeed, nor will a swing that is not backed up with a very long follow-through.


**Springing teal**
This is an old favourite, and is pretty typical of the way teal jump up off the water when taken by surprise. Very steeply rising, they are normally thrown as a simultaneous pair that fly away from the shooter.

Climbing as steeply as they do, the clays very soon lose their velocity and stall, after which they flop to the ground in a very un-teal like fashion. For this reason these clays have to be hit 'on the rise' or they usually will not count as 'kills' whatever the result of the shot.

Fortunately, these are among the less difficult targets, unless they have been set so they rise from a point a long way in front of the shooter. However, no matter how far away they happen to be the principle remains the same.

Normally, the targets will appear from above a hedge or protective shield and the muzzles should be pointed just there or slightly higher, with the stock in the 'ready' position.

When they rise the shooter must select his first target and begin pointing the muzzles up to it at the same time as he begins mounting the gun. The gun should come to the fully mounted position just before the muzzles catch the target, the swing continuing through it, and the shot fired. Forward allowance of some sort is required here but as usual the eyes must never leave the target. The amount of lead is probably no more than that necessary on an incoming, fairly low target.

When the first target has been shot the stock is slightly eased in the shoulder, the muzzles dropped back behind and on the line of the second and the whole thing repeated. Sadly, it is not as simple to put into practice as to describe!

The stance for this pair is not critical, although it is never good practice to stand in a sloppy fashion just because the target seems easy. That is the quick route to disappointment. Weight should be on the forward foot throughout both shots.

**Rabbits**
To many people's way of thinking these things would be better named 'kangaroos' since only rarely do they actually run along the ground. More often than not they bounce up in the air at every small bump and if that happens just as you shoot, tough luck!

Normally, the shooter has only a short time to see and shoot at these rabbit clays, rather like the real thing in fact. A typical layout might feature two sets of straw bales, perhaps only twenty yards apart, and it is between these that the targets will run.

Although they would seem quite easy, the rabbit stand can give a lot of trouble to some shooters. The swing-through method is the most frequently employed but this particular stand is tailor-made for sustained lead.

All you have to do is hold the gun a few yards out from where the rabbit will appear and, when it does, move the muzzles so that they stay ahead of it, firing as the gun hits the shoulder. The amount of forward allowance given is much more apparent when shooting sustained lead instead of swing-through and, on a rabbit target twenty yards away, this will be something in the order of three to four feet. Skeet shooters who are familiar with this method will soon adapt it to rabbits.

Regardless of the method you use, focus on the target. There are too many things around these particular targets which can distract the shooter who is not paying full attention, not the least of which is the ground itself, strewn with broken rabbits!

**The direct crossing pair**
The most important decision to make when taking this sort of double is which should be shot first. Here observation comes in useful. Before it is your turn to shoot, have a good look and see which target is ahead of the other at the point where the first shot is fired. It is highly unlikely that they will be absolutely side by side and the thing to do is select the rearmost target as the one to shoot first. This way there will be

no need to come back for the second target, having shot the first one. When the target has been shot the swing can just carry straight on to the second one, making any slight adjustments in elevation on the way.

For any pair of this type, it is always advantageous to stand favouring the two targets, but don't overdo it.

## The walk-up

These are not seen so often these days, probably because they take up so much room. This is a shame, since they can be very testing. The most usual sort of targets found on walk-up courses are those which fly away from the shooter, either directly or from the side. Other than in the unlikely event of the target springing up right at the shooter's feet these targets are all crossing shots to a greater or lesser degree and need to be shot accordingly. This entails starting with the muzzles just behind the target and swinging through it, however short this swing might need to be. The shallower the angle at which the target is flying, the less the swing that is necessary, but there must always be a swing of some sort. The gun should be mounted just as the target is caught and the shot fired without hesitation.

The actual process of walking down the course produces some strange, shuffling gaits, especially when the targets are released without warning. It is no good getting caught 'wrong footed' and many shooters will advance down these courses in short shuffles, keeping the foot from which they shoot in front all the time. Nothing wrong with that if it works.

## Targets from behind

In this shot the shooter is obliged to position himself with his back to the trap stand, usually by the design of the safety cage or because he is standing against a hedge or belt of trees. The target appears over his head flying away and often down as well, just for good measure. If they are high, too, they are far from easy.

Trying to shoot these by coming through the target from behind has a number of drawbacks. In this instance, starting behind means starting above and it will certainly mean that at the beginning of the swing the target will not be visible—which is distinctly unhelpful.

It is much better to keep the gun ahead of the target all the time, which in this case means starting under it and staying there.

Just how far under the target the muzzles must start depends on the height of the target and, to some extent, its speed. Very low targets of this kind may be treated just like the station one Skeet targets they resemble. More often, Sporting targets will be a good bit higher than this but, even so, the principle is almost the same.

For these higher ones, the shooter really needs to set himself up so that his 'ready' position resembles the finished position achieved when actually shooting at the ordinary incoming high tower target, that is, with the weight on the forward foot and the body arched back. It is rather uncomfortable, admittedly, but it is the only way possible to look back and up at the emerging target.

The muzzle position needs to be well up for this one, remembering that the idea is for them to be in such a position as to enable the shooter to go for the target the moment it appears.

The movement of the gun is unusual in this shot because the muzzles must obviously go down as the gun is being mounted, and not up or straight out. For that reason it is best to forget the normal 'ready' position of the stock: instead, hold it further out from the body. On this one some right-hand lift will not come amiss.

The object then is to start moving the muzzles down as the target appears, keeping them pointing at a spot in front of the target to give the necessary forward allowance. As this is a form of 'sustained lead' shooting, the lead given will be more apparent than when shooting swing-through.

Maintaining the forward allowance, the gun is mounted firmly, a brief moment is taken to check the lead, then with the gun still moving downwards ahead of the target the shot is fired. Do not forget to follow through!

The old problem of how much lead to give is something that the individual shooter must resolve for himself, of course, because it will vary substantially from shot to shot. In *actual* terms, the lead on this target will be zero on the Skeet-type shot and as much as several yards on the high tower.

### Doubles from behind

As can be seen from all the earlier sections, the shooting of doubles is a matter of shooting two singles in quick succession, the outcome being greatly affected by what happens during that brief period between the two shots. A high double like the target described is certainly to be numbered among the most difficult pairs with which the Sporting shooter is likely to be confronted and on any shoot this will be one of those stands which sorts the masters from the apprentices.

When the first target has been shot as described, the gun must be very slightly eased in the shoulder and face, but not removed from either. The muzzles are taken straight across to the second target, on its line and in front of it, and the shot repeated as for the first.

Since the angle of the second target will be different from the first, because it has gone further out, the perceived lead will probably be different, too.

### The straight 'going away' target

By most people's reckoning this one should be included under Basic Technique, but since it does give a lot of trouble to many otherwise competent shooters it has been put here with other more advanced targets.

At first sight it would appear to be the simplest shot of all, but during my early years as a shooting instructor it gradually dawned on me that this just was not so. Beginners, unless allowed to start with the gun mounted, always found this one particularly tricky and never really got the hang of it until they had learned and assimilated the basic arts of the shotgun.

Any target which goes directly away from the shooter, regardless of range, seems to just sit still in the sky, having no discernible movement across the shooter's vision. It becomes, therefore, the prime candidate for some careful aiming down the rib—but this never works!

The gunmount and timing on this shot has to be well-nigh perfect if the shot is to be successful, but beginners do not make perfect gunmounts and they have not yet learned good timing. For the more experienced shots the problem lies only with the way in which the gun is mounted, but this is a big 'only'! The main point here is not where the gun happens to end up in the shoulder and face, but how it gets there in the first place.

This is one shot where the Churchill 'ready' position really scores, because most trouble is caused with the shot when the stock is raised abruptly to the face. This leaves the muzzles pointing well under the target so that the gun has to be re-adjusted before the shot can be fired. It is here that aiming down the rib can easily occur.

From the recommended 'ready' position (stock tucked into the armpit) it is much easier to make the right move, which is to point the muzzles straight at the target as the stock is slid into the shoulder and face.

No chance of a mishap here! Sporting stand with cage; the target in this particular instance is flying almost straight away.

The gun should come to the fully mounted position, with the muzzles never leaving the target even for a moment, while the eyes, of course, must be focused hard on the target throughout. The shot must be fired the instant the stock beds firmly into the shoulder, no time being taken to try to 'make sure' by aiming along the rib.

The stance, as for almost every other shot, needs to be fairly narrow, with the weight forward on the front foot. A slight lean into the target is necessary to retain balance and this also will help make the shot a little more aggressive.

### Double 'going away'

The first target in this double is treated the same way as the single. For the second target, it is essential that the gun is brought right out of the shoulder so that the whole pointing movement may be repeated.

Attempting just to swing across to the second target instead of pointing the muzzles at it will often cause the shot to go to the side, so avoid doing this.

If there is a secret to mastering a very basic shot quickly, then it must be plenty of correct dry practice (see Training Methods on page 132).

### Silly targets

Some shoot organisers seem to delight in putting on the odd stand where the targets are just impossible. A good example was on display at a British Sporting Championship a few years ago, when a pair of so-called ducks got up at the very limits of sensible shotgun range and flew *away* from the shooter!

This sort of thing does no good to anyone and ruining a good score on a silly stand like this quite rightly upsets many people.

Such practice should be jumped on whenever the CPSA has a hand in the organisation, but unfortunately this does not always happen. If the good shots are frustrated by these kinds of targets, organisers should spare a thought for the poor old average shooters.

# FITASC Sporting

Sporting shot under FITASC rules is much closer to the real thing than is the English version as no two targets are ever the same. For those who are unfamiliar with its format, this is how it works.

Targets are shot in squads of six shooters in rounds of twenty-five targets each, every round featuring different targets from those encountered in any other round. In a one hundred target shoot, for instance, there will be four quite different 'stands', each with its own unique type of targets. On each stand there will be several traps, their positions and the targets they throw depending on the type of birds the stand is meant to represent. One stand of twenty-five might feature mainly high targets, whereas another might be entirely made up of 'rabbits'. Equally, it could be a combination of the two.

All the traps on each stand will throw a target or targets on their own fixed line, the variations of angle being altered by the squad moving to a number of designated shooting positions within the stand area. In this way, a pair of targets which in the first position were coming straight over might, in the second position, be going away and across. With five or six different trap positions per stand the possibilities are endless.

The order of shooting within the squad also changes for each new shooting position. At the first shooting position on stand A, for example, the order of shooting will be shooter number 1 first followed by shooters 2, 3, 4, 5 and 6. In the second shooting position the order becomes 2, 3, 4, 5, 6 and 1, and so on.

This is much better than in Skeet or Trap, where you are stuck with your squad position throughout the shoot, like it or not. The FITASC way, everyone gets a fair crack of the whip and no one feels cheated.

There are several drawbacks with this form of Sporting, however, not the least being its expense.

There are obviously far more actual shooting positions within the various stands, which requires many more traps and trappers than would be necessary at an equivalent English Sporting shoot. This, plus the cost of paid referees, soon adds to the costs, and ultimately the shooter has to cover the additional expense. A much larger area is also required to stage a full-scale FITASC sporting competition.

All this aside, most shooters would agree that it is the definitive form of Sporting shooting and probably the most testing form of clay shooting in existence. At the moment it is shot predominantly in just a few European countries and whether it ever catches on as a discipline shot world-wide remains to be seen. I hope it does.

## Conclusion

As I said at the beginning, this chapter is in no way comprehensive and it is unlikely, given the amount of available space, that it ever could have been.

Needless to say, there will be a few targets which do not quite slot in to any of the categories described here. Unfortunately, you will have to sort those out for yourself!

# 7
# Skeet Shooting

In an earlier chapter (Basic Technique) the so-called 'swing-through' shooting method was described. This method is the one successfully employed by the majority of Sporting clay shooters, all Trap shooters and a fair number of those who shoot Skeet. It is a simple and straightforward method but not, as most people imagine, the original or only method.

Anyone who has ever tried to shoot a moving target with a flintlock gun will have discovered one important fact: the gun does not actually shoot at the exact instant that you pull the trigger. This, of course, seriously disrupts the timing employed by the 'swing-through' method, and so obviously it cannot have been the method used in days gone by. Something else must have been used.

This 'something else' just happens to be a rather fine way of shooting any of the various Skeet disciplines and is known as the 'sustained lead' method.

The name is self-explanatory, I suppose, and means that the gun is actually pointed ahead of the target from the word go and is kept there throughout the swing. Exactly how far ahead of the target the muzzles have to be pointing is dependent on several factors: the speed of the target, its range, and the angle at which it is flying relative to the shooter.

In most forms of shotgun shooting this very necessary information (for sustained-lead shooting) is just not available and guesswork is a poor substitute. In Skeet shooting, however, all these factors are known and so the use of the sustained-lead method becomes a distinct possibility.

Many shooters, satisfied with the 'swing-through' method, might ask 'Why bother?' There are a number of good reasons.

With such predictable targets as those of Skeet, the exact lead required for each of them is easily learned. As a result shooting the sustained-lead method allows for very precise shooting of the targets.

Since the muzzles do not have to catch and pass any given target, the actual gun movement relative to that target is somewhat slower when using the sustained-lead method. It allows the shooter to take the target at the same point in the sky as he would with the 'swing-through' method, but with less effort and therefore more control, or conversely, to shoot the same target somewhat quicker using the same amount of effort.

This particular advantage shows best when shooting the international version of Skeet, where the targets are out and gone very quickly, making the shooting of doubles quite tricky. Obviously, the earlier the first target can be shot, the easier the second becomes and it is here that the 'sustained lead' method really helps.

Apart from the fact that the muzzles start ahead of the target instead of behind, all the familiar rules of good shotgun shooting still apply. The eyes must still be focused exclusively on the target, the gun must be mounted correctly and swung smoothly, etc.

Anyone wishing to try shooting this style will, initially, find it quite difficult to break old habits. Mounting the gun ahead of the target feels quite wrong to begin with and therefore it is probably best to start on something fairly easy like a station one or station seven incomer. The lead required by these two targets is no more than a foot and the way to tackle them is as follows.

Standing on station one the gun is held at the ready position, with the muzzles pointing over the target crossing point marker, or centre peg as it is known. When the low target appears the gun is mounted very steadily, the muzzles pointing at a spot several feet ahead of the target—how many does not matter as long as it is no more than about six or so. It is equally important that the muzzles are kept on the flightline of the target, not below it or above. The lead is adjusted as the gun is being mounted so that by the time the gun slots into the shoulder the lead of one foot has been established. During the whole operation, the eyes are kept glued to the target. After a momentary pause to check that the lead is correct, the gun is fired and the target should break.

This description of 'adjusting' the lead makes the whole thing sound a bit like rifle shooting but there must be no actual aiming involved. It is every bit as much a reflex action as 'swing-through', not a carefully studied one.

The same sequence can be repeated on station seven high target, and when both station one low and station seven high target can be handled easily then station two low and station six high can be tackled.

A more precise description of these and all the other skeet stations follows.

## Skeet, station by station

One of the problems of writing a book of instruction is deciding not what to put in but rather what to leave out. It would be quite possible, when describing Skeet in its various forms, to write something at considerable length, as there are numerous styles and approaches, all of which can have their fair share of success. However, this would lead to confusion for the would-be Skeet shooter and to considerable dismay from the publishers! Therefore, this chapter will describe the method used by the vast majority of the world's leading Skeet shooters in both the domestic and international forms of the game, being a combination of the best aspects of the swing-through and sustained-lead methods. It is a method I have observed and used over a period of eleven years.

The reason for the use of the sustained-lead method has already been explained; the use of the swing-through method on certain targets is from necessity rather than choice, its inclusion being unavoidable on the second target of some of the doubles. However, this is no bad thing, since circumstances sometimes dictate that these second targets cannot be shot exactly the way the Skeet shooter would wish, making them a little less 'readable' than the singles and therefore more easily shot with the swing-through method.

I make no excuses for choosing to describe international Skeet rather than its domestic counterparts, although I hasten to add that it is in no way intended to infer that I consider the domestic forms unworthy of mention, far from it. International Skeet is not *so* different from the domestic forms and for this reason several pages have been included at the end of the chapter so that the shooter can adjust the analysis to suit his favourite discipline.

Within the limitations imposed by the size of this book there were two options. One was to include every discipline and its variations in a scanty form which would lead nowhere; the other was to pick just a few of the disciplines and to describe each chosen in detail, with the object of providing a more comprehensive analysis. This, in turn, would permit the shooter to glean sufficient information which he could then apply to any discipline that fell within the guidelines of the ones described.

Domestic Skeet has been adequately covered in a number of books, none of which were written in Britain, but, as far as I know, no one in this or any other country has put the techniques of ISU Skeet in book form.

## Shooting International Skeet

Before any would-be ISU Skeet shooter tries his first round or two at this discipline there are a number of things which should be observed. Firstly, it is probably a waste of time attempting this form of Skeet until the shooter can exhibit a certain skill with the gun, preferably on something like English Sporting at a local club. ISU Skeet, like Olympic Trap, is not the discipline on which to cut your clay shooting teeth.

Assuming, then, that the shooter is already relatively proficient, it is essential from the very beginning that he acquaints himself with the required but rather awkward ISU Skeet ready position. It is a very unnatural position, for the rules require that part of the gunstock touches the hipbone, and to ensure that this rule is being observed the shooter's clothing is appropriately marked so the officials can keep a check.

Some countries school their referees to be particularly keen on the correct ISU Skeet position and invariably a few shooters get caught out when shooting in these places. Theoretically, at least, the jury may impose the ultimate penalty of deducting targets from the score of a persistent offender, although I have never actually witnessed such an occurrence. However, there can be nothing more distracting or more certain to break concentration than to be stopped mid-round by the referee and warned about gun position!

The answer, of course, is to learn the correct position from day one of your Skeet-shooting career so that it soon becomes second nature to position the gun properly.

## Beginning the round

In any sport no competitor worth his salt is ever entirely nerve-free and it is undesirable that he should be. This nervousness is a form of combat readiness, essential if maximum performance is to be achieved. In a 'fight or flight' situation the body is charged with adrenalin, vision is better and the reflexes are that much sharper.

No shooter in my experience has ever actually made a run for it when confronted with the prospect of shooting a round of Skeet, but many look as though they are seriously considering it!

Amazingly negative and quite unwarranted fears can flood the mind of even the most able shooter on occasion. He may well have shot the last fifty rounds perfectly but what about *this* one? Such 'non-thinking' afflicts all of us at times and the only way to combat it is to ensure that everything is absolutely right before the round actually begins.

Probably nothing is more important than to have a good start, which means hitting that first target on station one. Most of us find that this reduces the heart-beat level considerably!

In competition, this station has to be shot 'cold' more often than not, the shooter not having fired the gun for several hours or maybe since the day before. A sound idea is to follow the routine adopted by the large majority of shooters immediately before a round, and that is to warm up with a series of practice swings at imaginary targets on various stations. For some reason, most people do this on station four, three, and two, in that order, although any station will do just as well. It certainly helps relax shooters, but it should not be carried to extremes in case fatigue sets in. The few minutes usually available before each round should suffice.

Under the rules, prior to the commencement of each round, each shooter is permitted to fire two shots to 'clear the gun'. Whilst virtually every Olympic Trap shooter follows such practice it is something seldom indulged in by the majority of Skeet shooters. Personally, I have never seen the point of it but some people feel comforted by letting the gun off in this fashion—it is a matter of personal taste.

Where you actually point the gun when firing these two shots is up to you so long as it is safe. However, officials take a rather dim view of anyone who blows one of their target limit markers out of the ground, so point the gun somewhere else, please.

The last thing before the round actually gets going is the viewing of the targets. Each squad is allowed to see one target from each house so that speed, elevation and direction can be observed. Have a good look. Although the targets will have been carefully set by the jury early in the morning, conditions change. A gradually freshening wind can alter target trajectories quite considerably, causing the targets variously to dip, rise, or swerve in flight. Unless the targets are a *long* way off track, the jury will not alter them. Have a good look at both of them.

Bruno Rossetti of France shows a relaxed, but alert, ready position and stance. Shooting the high target on station six.

**Station one**
Unless you happen to be number one on the squad, have a look at the targets of the shooter immediately preceding you to make sure they are the same as those viewed. If they are not, then you must stay very alert to variations which might occur on any station.

The foot position as shown in the top diagram on page 83 is suitable for anyone starting Skeet, although the shooter can gradually adapt this if necessary as his style develops. The feet should be no more than shoulder-width apart.

The ISU ready position is assumed, with the barrels pointing upwards at an angle of 35-40° to the ground and on the line of the viewed target. This will usually mean the barrels being aligned over the centre peg (the target crossing point).

The rules permit a practice gunmount on this station. Many shooters use this as a rehearsal of the target to be shot but it is not essential and some of the best shooters never do it. Try it and see which you prefer.

The eyes should hold a soft focus just above the muzzles; be careful not to allow them to focus on the muzzles themselves. It is also a bad idea to look a long way above the barrels with the idea of seeing the target earlier. This tends to make the shooter jump at the target and try to take it too soon.

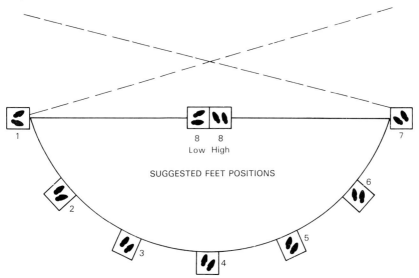

Skeet range diagram showing feet positions (the stations are 3' x 3').

KEY ...... high house hold positions
_____ low house hold positions
•—•— lines along which correct dimensions are ascertained

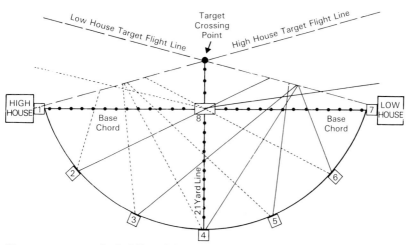

Skeet range muzzle 'hold' positions.

Once the shooter is set up in the address position and ready, he calls for the target.

Unless the target is flying much higher than usual (unlikely unless a strong headwind has sprung up since the targets were set by the jury) it always seems to be dropping from the moment it appears. No compensatory action by the shooter is necessary, for the relatively high muzzle position at address will ensure that as the gun is mounted a slight dipping action of the muzzles is built-in, thus preventing the shot from going high.

All the shooter has to do, as the target appears, is focus on the target, point the muzzles straight at it with the left hand, and raise the stock to the shoulder and face with the right. This must be a smooth, unhurried action, although with the target whizzing away it takes confidence and some practice to achieve. The gun *must* be fired the instant the stock beds firmly into position. Hanging on to 'make sure' will almost certainly guarantee that the target will be missed.

Observing top shooters taking this target, it is easy to be misled into thinking that because they take the target so early they must be moving very quickly. It is an illusion, as close attention to the shooter rather than the target will soon prove: a steady gunmount in combination with the immediate firing of the gun as the mount occurs—that's the secret.

*Possible errors*

This target is missed for a number of reasons:

1 Reacting to the sound of the trap instead of waiting to see the target. Although reacting this way can result in some very early and spectacular hits, the target will be missed if it does not go exactly where the shooter expects. Wait to see it before moving—there is time.

2 Raising the gun too abruptly with the right hand. This causes the muzzles to dip excessively and the shot will go under the target. A smooth unhurried movement is what is wanted, with the two hands working in unison.

3 Failure to mount the gun fully to the shoulder and face. Invariably, when this sort of mismount occurs, the shooter is uncomfortably aware that at the moment of pulling the trigger he is unable to see the target. It is beneath the barrels and the shot goes right over the top. Trying to mount too fast can cause the error, so take it easy! It is worth noting that in the correct shot the target is in view all the time.

There can be no doubt, regardless of the three points just cited, that far and away the commonest cause for missing *any* target is the shooter not watching it properly. At all times the eyes must be focused totally on the target; not partly on the gun or bead; not on the target and all the rest of the world around it; just the target.

Good shotgun shooting is guided by instinct and conditioned reflex action, a multitude of small but significant muscular movements dictated entirely by what the eyes see. The more concentrated the focus, the more concentrated and accurate will be the resulting muscular reactions.

The ability of a shooter to give his full attention to the target, both visually and mentally, will largely determine the level to which he can ultimately aspire.

## Station one, double

Shooting the double on this station should cause no problems to any shooter who can handle the high house single with any degree of confidence. Quite simply, the first target of the double is shot in exactly the same fashion as the single. It might almost be said that the single targets are shot in such a way as to serve as a rehearsal for the doubles to come.

Beginners get slightly panicky when shooting doubles because they feel that there is not enough time, so they rush the first shot and make a mess of it. This is not necessary, because here there is plenty of time.

Most shooters will find that as they shoot the high house single, their weight will automatically transfer slightly to the front foot. This is desirable but must not be so excessive as to allow the shooter to lose balance.

In the double the same thing applies. The high target is shot as described for the single, slightly before it reaches the centre peg. Having shot this first target correctly, the incoming low house target will be just passing the centre peg and will be seen slightly to the left of the barrels. Keeping the weight just favouring the front foot, the muzzles are moved after the second target until they overtake it and swing through. The shot is fired when the muzzles have just passed the target, a lead of around 1½ ft being required by those who actually see lead. The target is quite well in towards the high house when it is shot. There is nothing to be gained by attempting to shoot this target earlier.

Executed properly, the swing at the second target is very much a turn of the body combined with correct use of the hands and arms. It must not be allowed to turn into a twisting movement as this will cause all sorts of problems. (See Training Methods on page 132.)

It is worth mentioning here that the gun is not removed from the shoulder between shots on this or any other Skeet double. Strongly recommended for game shooting, such a dismount has no place on the Skeet field. All that is required is a relaxing of muscular tension immediately after the first shot, which will allow a smooth swing at the second target. The relaxing should not be conscious, rather it should be something which will eventually occur naturally.

### Possible errors

For most shooters, even newcomers to Skeet, once the high target is shot all the problems should be over. The station one low target is probably the least missed target on the Skeet field but sometimes it does slip by. However, even the Skeet neophyte is rarely a shooter in the early stages of his clay shooting career so that if he misses this target, having hit the first, it can only really be excused by lack of attention, or by having taken the target for granted.

Sometimes even quite experienced shooters find that while they can handle the high house single target, it gets away from them when they shoot it in the double. Since the high target is identical in the single and the double there are few possible answers. One, and unlikely in an experienced shot, is that of rushing the target. Far more likely, though, is that the shooter is unconsciously allowing his eyes to leave the target before it has actually been shot. He is probably looking too soon for the second target of the double.

A little secret here and on all doubles is to see the first target actually break before looking for the second.

## Station two: high house single

If there were to be a vote among Skeet shooters to decide the least popular target on the field it is a sure bet that this one would poll more than its fair share. By no means the most technically difficult it is, nevertheless, the first of the 'missable' targets encountered during a round and catches the shooter when he is still rather tight and nervous.

The biggest problem with the target is that it looks much more difficult than it actually is and many shooters, particularly Skeet novices, find themselves intimidated by it. Fortunately, if the shooter goes about it the right way, this target is no more difficult than any other.

A good set-up at address is essential. Hold and feet positions can be varied slightly from the illustrations on page 83, but not too much. Some strange stances are sometimes seen on this station, many of them born from desperation rather than efficacy, and these are best avoided. The basic stance as shown in the photograph on page 82 applies to all stations, with the possible exception of station eight, and twisting oneself into contortions reminiscent of Quasimodo will not help at all!

As with station one, the feet should be no more than shoulder-width apart, with the weight just favouring the leading foot in a ratio of about 55%-45%. The legs should be comfortably relaxed and slightly bent at the knees to encourage free movement.

Adopting the ISU ready position, with the toe of the stock just touching the hipbone, the shooter will find that the position in which he is standing will cause the gun to be pointed just left of the centre peg, the position where, ideally, the target will be broken.

To get into actual address position the body must now be turned at the hips until the muzzles are facing a point slightly to the right of parallel with the face of the high house. The actual height of the muzzles should be such that they sit, as the shooter sees them, just below the anticipated flightline of the target. Notice that this does not mean that the barrels are actually *pointing* below the flightline. They will be pointing a good deal higher than this. It is just that to the shooter's eye the muzzles themselves are below the flightline.

This is a good position although, it must be admitted, many of the finest shooters bring the muzzles closer to the house while others do the opposite. It all really depends on how early the individual sees the target. By this I mean *really* sees it: clearly focused and not just as a flash streaking across the sky! It is no good at all trying to shoot at a blur, since the resulting shot can and does go anywhere. However, regard the position described as a good place from which to experiment.

Like the gun position at address, there are no hard-and-fast rules as to where the shooter should actually look when waiting for the target. One thing is for certain, though. The target exit window is definitely *not* the place to look, and there are two reasons for this. One is that the target will flash across the shooter's vision and then will at best be focused very late, and two is that in order to look into the window the head must be turned considerably out of its ideal position relative to the gun.

The best place to look, for most shooters, is mid-way between the house and the muzzles, taking care not to allow the eyes to focus on a distant tree or cloud. Once all of these preliminaries are taken care of (which fortunately takes much less time to do than to read!), the target can be called.

Sometime between the shooter calling and the permitted three seconds elapsing, the target will emerge. The shooter must remain physically relaxed but mentally very alert, ready for action.

As the target leaves the house the shooter will detect its presence via his peripheral vision so that by the time it actually comes properly into his field of view he will already have it in focus. The correct time to begin the swing movement is as soon as the shooter sees that the target (in his peripheral vision) has emerged from the house. It is too late if the target is allowed to reach and pass the muzzles, since this target is to be shot utilising the sustained lead method. The shooter must begin moving the muzzles ahead of the target at the same time as he is turning his body and commencing the gunmount. (This movement is described under Training Methods on page 132.)

The shooter will be aware that the muzzles are leading the target by about a foot and as the gun is bedded into the face and shoulder the shot is fired without hesitation, the target breaking a yard or so before it reaches the centre peg.

There is a limited amount of follow-through on this shot because it is flying as much away as across and does not therefore require a big swing.

Watching good Skeet shooters taking this target, it will be noticed that they take it in the same place every time, practically to the inch. On the double this sets up the second target perfectly.

*Possible errors*

To attempt to list all the ways that this target can be missed could fill a small book and would only cause confusion. However, here are a few tips:

1  Do not try and 'make sure' of this one—you will only make sure that you miss it. As soon as the gun settles in the shoulder and face, shoot.

2  Do not try to be too spectacular. Blowing the target to dust when it is only twenty feet from the traphouse looks very impressive when it works but will also mean a lot of missed targets. Remember, it is how many you break that counts, not how quickly!

3  When things go wrong check that the basics are correct or seek informed assistance. Do not be tempted into weird experiments.

## Station two: low house single

One of the so-called easy targets, this is one of those that should certainly never be missed. Good shooters do miss it, however, and when they do they feel like kicking themselves because they know that they have, in effect, just given the rest of the competitors a target.

The stance and weight distribution are the same as for the high house target. The only difference is that now the muzzles are directed over station eight, and held just below the target flightline.

Seeing this one is no problem unless there is a background uncomplimentary to the target colour, and even then only a sleepy shooter will fail to see it coming.

When the target is called and it emerges the gun is immediately set in motion but without any rush. As the gun is being mounted it is kept ahead of the target, the lead at the same time being adjusted to 2-2½ ft. Maintaining this lead, the gun is fully mounted. It is not necessary to fire the instant the gun hits the shoulder and, in fact, many shooters prefer to let the gun swing for a few yards before actually firing, being careful, of course, not to allow the gun to slow or stop. This 'riding' of the target, as it is known, allows the shooter to have a quick check before committing himself to the shot.

It must essentially remain a reflex action, however, and not be allowed to deteriorate into something akin to a carefully aimed rifle shot!

Having fired and broken the target, the follow-through will finish with the muzzles pointing almost to the high house.

*Possible errors*

Not too much to go wrong here, and the majority of misses can be attributed to lack of attention. Often, the shooter takes the high target and, having broken it, mentally relaxes. This can sometimes mean that the shooter gives the low target virtually no attention at all and on it goes, unbroken.

The novice Skeet shooter can, of course, miss anything, including this target and probably the most common error here is that of falling away from the target instead of turning with the weight still on the forward foot. When this happens the swing tends to slow and the muzzles rise upwards with obvious results. Keep the weight on the forward foot and turn; do not twist.

## Station two: double

As in the case of station one, if you can hit the singles you can hit the double.

The first target of this double is the one from the high house and the address position is exactly the same as for the single. The one major difference is that now there are two targets in the air simultaneously instead of just one, but this fact must be ignored. Only one target can be shot at a time and there is sufficient time to shoot both without the shooter having to jump out of his boots to do it!

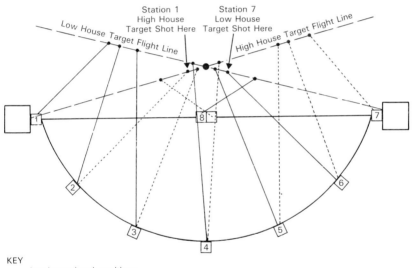

KEY
_____ low house break positions
...... high house break positions

Skeet range diagram showing where the target should be broken from each station.

With this in mind the first target of the double is shot in just the same fashion as the single, no faster. As soon as the target is seen to break (or is seen to fly on untouched), then the attention is switched to the second one.

Having shot or shot at the outgoing high target the second will appear just to the left of the muzzles, heading in the opposite direction. Here the 'swing-through' method is once again utilised. The swing is reversed, the target is passed and when the lead is correct the shot is fired, the gun not being allowed to stop until the muzzles are pointing in the vicinity of the high house. This sort of follow-through may seem excessive but it does ensure that the gun is still moving as the shot is fired.

*Possible errors*

Once the high house single can be handled reasonably well the double should create few problems.

Avoid lifting the face off the stock when shooting the second target and do not fall back, but keep the weight on the forward foot.

## Station three: high house single

Progressing further round the Skeet field this is the first of the true crossing targets and one where the real speed of the ISU targets is first experienced. To my mind, it is here that the sustained lead method really comes into its own, turning a difficult station into something which, whilst never actually easy, is certainly somewhat easier. Granted, many good Skeet shooters employ the 'swing-through' method when they shoot this target but it is harder work, and looks it.

Stance and balance are the same as for station two high house, the weight slightly forward and the muzzles held just below the target flightline. The position of the feet should be about that as shown previously. The address position, relative to the high house, is determined by the reaction speed of the shooter concerned. It will tend to get faster as the shot becomes more of a conditioned reflex action, but in the beginning a good starting point is to have the muzzles positioned so that they are pointing mid-way between the high house and the centre peg.

One point to bear in mind on all stations is that, where the fast outgoing targets are concerned, the shooter should always position himself in such a way that he is *forced* to react aggressively in order to stay ahead of the target. Positioning the muzzles so that a casual, easy start is possible will result in these targets being shot too late or missed altogether.

The place to look for the target is just outside the right edge of the house, level with the target window. Once again, looking into the window is wrong! The target is called for only when the shooter is absolutely ready, because inattention will allow this one to be halfway across the field before the shooter moves.

As soon as the target is seen to emerge the muzzles must be pushed out ahead of it, the body turn and gun mount commencing simultaneously. The exact movement is described under Training Methods on page 133.

Before the gun is completely mounted the lead will have been adjusted to from 3-4 ft, so that when the gun finally slots firmly into the shoulder and face the shot can be fired immediately. The follow-through should continue almost as far as the low house.

Ideally, the target will be broken on or slightly before the centre peg, although achieving this is something that most newcomers to Skeet initially will find to be quite beyond them. However, with constant dry mounting practice, combined with actual rounds of Skeet, it will eventually sort itself out. Essentially, aim as much for smoothness as speed during these sessions, and bear in mind during practice that while the target is much easier if it is shot three or four yards later, this is no use at all when shooting doubles!

The business of adjusting the lead may suggest that there is some consultation of the muzzle position by the eyes and that the shot is executed in a deliberate and studied way. This is not so. It would be impossible to achieve in the time available (about ¾ of a second on this target).

The eyes, as for all shots, must be focused only on the target, nowhere else. The mind must be programmed to do what is necessary before the target is called and then the shooter must turn the whole operation over to his conditioned reflexes.

Of course, in the early stages the shooter will not *have* conditioned reflexes. Most of what he does on the Skeet field will have to be done consciously and, as a result, will be slow and somewhat inaccurate. Such are the joys of learning a new discipline!

Fortunately, with some diligent practice, the shooter soon comes to appreciate what is required and his shooting will rapidly improve.

*Possible errors*
Like station two, there are all sorts of ways of missing this target. The following are major points on which to concentrate.

1 Make sure when calling for the target that you are *really* ready, even if the target were to come at the instant of your call. Some quite experienced Skeet shooters call for the target while still settling themselves on the station. This can only serve to make a hard target even harder.

2 The weight must remain over the front foot throughout the shot and follow-through. Fire and fall back will not work.

3 As with the high house two target, do not try for the spectacular shot. For every cloud of dust left hanging in the sky just a few yards out of the house, there will be a complete miss—it is not worth it.

4 As with all targets, correct elevation of the shot is every bit as important as the direction. Strive during actual shooting and dry practice to maintain control over the muzzles, ensuring that they are kept on the flightline of the real or imaginary target through the swing and follow-through.

5 It is important that the foot position is not varied too much. It is tempting to stand with the feet turned in a more clockwise direction so that the shooter is facing more towards the low house. While this certainly makes

it easier to swing the gun, the movement becomes very much one of the hands and arms only, with the body practically stationary. Although it may feel quite good it really is not, particularly when trying to shoot the low house target in the double.

### Station three: low house single

A deceptive target, this one is more tricky than it appears to be, not least because it happens to be one of the longest shots encountered during a round of Skeet. Consequently, it requires more lead than one imagines.

The stance, foot position and weight distribution are the same as for the high target, although this time the barrels are pointed between the centre peg and the low house. As with most of the other targets the muzzles (as they are seen by the shooter) are held just below the target flightline.

The place to look for the target is to the left of the target window, just beyond the outside edge of the house. Be careful if the background is similar to the target colour. If this one gets a five-yard start on you it can be suddenly quite difficult.

The target is called and the muzzles are moved off ahead of it as soon as it appears. The lead picture is adjusted to about four feet as the gun is being brought smoothly to the face and shoulder. When the gun is fully mounted, a fraction of a second is allowed to check that everything is correct, then the shot is fired and the shooter follows-through. To assist a continuous movement during the shot the follow-through should finish at or near the high house.

Although not by any means a shot that should be hurried, it must not be allowed to go *too* far down the field! Ideally, it will be broken when it is about three or four yards beyond the centre peg.

Although rated as one of the less difficult targets, this one just happens to be missed more often than an 'easy' target should be. Obviously, it is not as easy as we all tend to think!

> *Possible errors*
> 1 Slowing the swing is very common on this target and probably accounts for the majority of misses. Maintain the lead and follow-through.
>
> Points 2, 3 and 4 of the high house target errors apply equally to this one.
> 5 Pay particular attention whenever the target has a tail wind. If the wind is at all strong the target can dip unexpectedly once it has passed the centre peg. Under these conditions the wise shooter will try to break the target a little earlier than usual.

### Station three: double

As with all doubles the first target is simply a repeat of the single, in this case the one from the high house. As with the single, the target must be broken on or before the centre peg but that does not mean it has to be shot *too* fast. It must be taken with the same tempo or rhythm as if it were the single.

Having shot the target in the correct place (and seen it break), the incoming low house target will be seen just left of the muzzles, heading quite rapidly in the opposite direction. This one must be shot with the 'swing-through' method.

The swing is reversed and, with the weight favouring the front foot, the muzzles are swung through the target and the shot fired, once the correct lead is seen. The follow-through must continue to the high house to avoid any tendency to slow or stop the swing. There must be no loss of balance during any part of this double.

*Possible errors*
Any of those cited for the singles, of course, plus a few extras.
1  If trouble with the high house target mostly occurs when shooting the double, take special care to watch the target *break* before looking for that second one.
2  If experiencing problems with the second target, particularly if this is a result of taking the target persistently later than is ideal, it is often necessary to look to the first target for the cure. Work this out for yourself.

**Station four**
Because there is no double on the station, many shooters tend to underestimate its difficulty. As these targets are among the most frequently missed on the Skeet field, they obviously warrant some care.

The mistake is to take them too slowly, trying to 'make sure', but this approach does not work well on any target and certainly not on these two.

**Station four: high house target**
Virtually a repeat of the station three high house target, the foot position is as illustrated. Of course, with no double to worry about the foot position can, theoretically, be anything that is comfortable, but this must not be taken to extremes.

Stance and balance are the same as for all other targets, the weight favouring the forward foot and the feet no more than shoulder-width apart.

In the address position the muzzles are held just below the target flightline and are pointed mid-way between the high house and the centre peg. As with station three, it is possible to bring the muzzles closer to the house than this (if your reactions are fast enough, that is), but it is not recommended that they be allowed to point further out from the house. Doing the latter will make the movement of the gun more of a stab than a swing and this sort of shot can go anywhere.

The place to look is to the right of the target window, just outside the edge of the high house.

Top Italian Skeet shooter, Lucca Scribani, prepares to take a high house target from station four.

The target comes out just as sharply as the high house target of the previous station, so stay alert when calling for it!

The instant the target is seen the swing must be set in motion so that the muzzles may be kept ahead throughout the shot. As the gun is being swung and mounted the lead is adjusted to about four feet and the shot is fired as the stock beds firmly into the shoulder and face. A good follow-through is essential and should only stop when the shooter can turn no further. Without getting tied up in knots, it will be when the gun is pointing in the vicinity of the low house. For safety reasons the gun must not be allowed to swing beyond this point anyway.

Shot correctly, the target will be broken on or just beyond the centre peg.

> *Possible errors*
> Everything said about the station three high house target applies here. Remember also, do not allow the gun to ride this one down the range, for you will miss it.

## Station four: low house target

A common mistake here is to shoot the high house target and then call immediately for this one—it is a big mistake! It must always be borne in mind that this station four low house target is the first *fast* low house target encountered in a round of Skeet and it is therefore not to be taken casually.

The address position should be quite familiar by now. Stance is about the same as for the high house target. Having said that, it must be pointed out that most experienced shots will actually shift from this position after shooting the high house target, before re-settling themselves again in the same position.

The purpose of this is to give the shooter time to clear his mind of the target just shot and to prepare himself for the next one. Also, it overcomes any tendency to rush the second target. (On every station, most experienced Skeet shooters have a slight pause for thought between single targets.)

The muzzles should be pointed mid-way between the low house and the centre peg and should be held just below the target flightline. The shooter's gaze should be directed to the left of the target window, just outside the edge of the house.

This target is shot with the sustained lead method. Therefore, as soon as it appears, the swing must commence and the muzzles be moved off ahead of it. The lead is adjusted to about four feet and as the gun beds firmly into position the shot is fired, the follow-through continuing to the high house. This target should be broken on or just beyond the centre peg.

*Possible errors*

1 Background plays some part in the shooting of this target. Because it starts so low it comes out invariably against a background of fields, trees or whatever else happens to be there. If the target and the background are of similar shades then look very carefully. Seeing it for the first time as it steams past the centre peg is no good!

2 A common error is to take the target by just dragging the gun across the body with the hands, instead of turning properly. This does not work too well.

3 Another common problem, and hard to detect yourself, is that of lifting the head off the stock before the shot is fired. This can often happen when the target is being buffeted by the wind.

    If you are suffering from inexplicable misses on the target, try concentrating on keeping your face firmly on the stock until after the follow-through is completed. This will often effect a cure.

## Station five

Having negotiated the first half of the Skeet field we arrive at what is probably the most technically difficult station of them all. When you can shoot this station easily then you can fairly reckon to be a real Skeet shooter!

## Station five: high single

Although this target is an incomer, and therefore to be rated among the 'easier' targets, it comes in fairly fast. It is especially tricky if it is wind-assisted, and it has the distinction of being the most frequently missed incomer on the Skeet field.

Watching someone else shoot the target, it looks quite innocent until you get on the receiving end of it, whereupon it appears to put on a bit of a spurt. Do not be caught out. It really is a target which must be shot as aggressively as any other target on the Skeet field.

With these thoughts in mind, set up in the usual stance, with the feet in the position as illustrated. The muzzles are held just below the target flightline and pointed mid-way between the centre peg and the high house.

Look just outside the edge of the house, level with the target window. The moment the target appears the gun must start moving, the muzzles staying ahead all the time. This one is deceptively fast, although in the initial stages of its flight it looks to be travelling quite slowly.

The lead should be a minimum of four feet and it should be adjusted as the gun is being mounted. Ideally, the gun will be firmly mounted just after the target has passed the centre peg, whereupon the shot should be fired without hesitation. It is not a target to 'ride' down the range!

If the prevailing wind is behind the target, a great deal of dipping and diving can occur, so it is best to shoot this one a little earlier in these sorts of conditions.

A good follow-through is essential and should finish with the gun pointing almost at the low house.

*Possible errors*
1  It is worth remembering that the target is rarely missed in front. Giving the target a bit of extra lead never does any harm.
2  The gun must remain firmly mounted throughout the shot and follow-through; lifting the head must be avoided.
3  Keep the weight on the front foot; do not fall back.

**Station five: low house single**
While the station two high house target is probably the most disliked target on the field, the honours for the most missed target must go to this one, regardless of the level of the shooters concerned.

Apart from the fact it appears to be very quick, the background is often a problem and setting up for it can fairly be said to be critical.

Stance and foot position are as for that of the high target, with the weight just favouring the leading foot.

At the address the muzzles should be pointed mid-way between the low house and the centre peg, and held just below the target flightline. With practice it is possible to bring the muzzles closer to the house than this, which will mean the target can be shot slightly quicker. However, only attempt this when the target begins to feel easy.

The place to look is just outside the edge of the house, level with the target window. Because of the invariably awkward background, be careful that the eyes only hold a 'soft' focus in this area.

Having assumed the correct position, the next thing is to call for the target. Only do so when absolutely ready. To shoot the high house target and then casually turn and call for this one will probably earn you a well-deserved miss. Shoot the high target, then wait for a second.

Get that target out of your mind . . . shuffle your feet a little if you like . . . then settle down and concentrate on this low one.

When the target appears move quickly but smoothly off ahead of it, adjusting the lead to about 3½ ft as the gun is being mounted. The gun must bed firmly into position just before the target reaches the centre peg and the shot fired without hesitation. The follow-through must continue almost to the high house.

*Possible errors*
1  All the problems that can occur on station four low target must be guarded against here, too. Unlike station four, however, this one *must* be shot over the centre peg at the very latest.
2  Be particularly aware of the muzzle height at address. Holding the muzzles too high is a common error which will tend to make the shot go low.
3  Do not fall towards the target as you shoot. This is not the target on which to lose balance! This sort of action is very natural but must be avoided, especially with regard to the double, when such movement would make the second target almost impossible.

**Station five: double**
As with all stations, if you can hit the singles then you can hit the double.

Shooting the first target, the low one, is a matter of repeating the action used for the low single, except that the follow-through must be abbreviated and the swing reversed the moment the target is seen to break. It is here that good weight distribution is so important. Over-committing the weight to the leading foot makes it hard to get back for the second target.

Having shot the first target in good balance, the second target must be pursued with a fair degree of aggression and determination. A casual swing will not catch it! This target is shot with the 'swing-through' method, the required lead being a minimum of four feet, and a good follow-through is essential.

*Possible errors*
1  Observation plays a big part in the successful negotiation of the station. With a tail wind, for instance, the high target will be diving quite a lot by the time the shooter catches it when shooting the double. Having missed it, it is no good complaining about this fact if the shooters immediately preceding you have had exactly the same sort of targets to contend with.
2  Four feet is given as the nominal lead for the high target: it can be broken with a good deal more, but never with less. Experiment.

3 On the occasions that the high target is flying into a head wind it slows down, giving the impression that it requires less lead. Do not be fooled—it still needs plenty.

4 Always bear in mind that trouble with the high target of this double is often caused by some sort of miscue in the execution of the low one, even though it may be breaking.

Austrian Skeet team in training (Grand Prix of Nations, Montecatini).

**Station six**
Having successfully negotiated the last station, the shooter must beware of mentally relaxing on this one. Station six is like station two in reverse and only causes less trouble because the shooter has warmed up by the time he reaches it. It still demands full concentration.

**Station six: high house single**
One of the simpler targets, this one is again shot with sustained lead. Stance is as normal, and at address the muzzles should point over station eight and be held slightly below the target flightline.

Where to look is not critical here as the background is usually sky, although it is still better not to look straight into the target window.

When the target appears the swing begins, steadily moving the muzzles ahead of the target as the gun is being mounted. Having adjusted the lead to about 2½ ft, the stock should come to the fully mounted position just as the target passes the centre peg. A slight pause as the gun 'rides' the target for a fraction of a second, then the shot is fired. Follow through!

*Possible errors*
Not too much to go wrong here. Be careful in a tail wind, though: the target should then be shot slightly earlier before it has a chance to dive under the barrels.

## Station six: low house single

As already mentioned, this target does not cause so many problems as its brother on station two.

The correct stance is that of all the other stations, foot position as illustrated. The muzzles should be held pointing slightly left of parallel with the house and, as usual, be held just below the target's flightline.

The key to the target is knowing where and how to look for it. Look back into the target window and you will never see it go. Stare at the background and the same thing will happen. A soft focus must be held in the area of the target's initial flight, although the actual position varies considerably among top shooters. Some look for this target as far out as the muzzles: it is a matter of finding what suits best.

When the target appears the muzzles must be kept ahead of it as the gun is being mounted, the shot being fired just before or over the centre peg. Lead on this one is only about a foot, no more, and the follow-through is relatively little.

*Possible errors*
1  Never shoot the target by relying on hearing the trap go off. Any sudden sound will trigger an unwanted reaction on the part of the shooter, and there are plenty of sudden sounds at a shooting competition! Having made a false start, the target inevitably zips out as the shooter is struggling to regain composure. It is a good case for wearing earmuffs and plugs.
2  As with all outgoing targets, shooting this one super-fast is very spectacular but too many will get away. Remember, it's not how fast, it's how many!

## Station six: double

The stance and address position are exactly the same as for the low single. The low target, the first to be shot in the double, is shot in just the same way as if it were the single, and as soon as the target is seen to break the swing is reversed. If the target has been shot in the right place the second will be picked up just to the right of the muzzles. Maintaining good balance, the shooter must swing the gun up to and through the target, firing when a lead of about 2½ ft is obtained. Do not forget to follow through.

*Possible errors*
1  Everything said about the singles applies equally in the double.

   2  In a tail wind the high target can be particularly tricky.
       Expect it to be diving.
   3  Having shot the low one, do not relax. The second cannot
       be taken for granted.

## Station seven
No singles on this station, just a double, and a simple one at that. Most mistakes on this pair occur through carelessness, although the low target can prove troublesome in a high wind. It also has to be watched if the targets are varying in their line of throw. Reacting to the sound of the trap instead of the sight of the target is asking for trouble, too.

The stance is as normal, with the muzzles aligned with the anticipated flightline of the first target to be shot, the low one. The height of the muzzles should be such that the target can be seen just above them as the gun is being mounted. They must not be held so high that the target slips out underneath them.

Once the target appears the muzzles must be pointed straight at it and the gun fired as soon as the stock is firmly bedded in position in the shoulder and face. Although breaking it over the centre peg is soon enough, most people find that without hurrying they can shoot the target rather earlier than this. It usually means that the muzzles will be pointing ahead of the second target when the swing is reversed, which means that it can be shot with sustained lead. The forward allowance is no more than 1½ ft and the target should be broken about mid-way between the centre peg and the low house.

If the target has to be shot 'swing-through', then this is also no problem. Either way, do not let the swing stop until the target has been seen to break.

*Possible errors*
   1  Trying to shoot the outgoer too fast will disrupt the timing
       of the shot. Also, it can mean that the stock is raised very
       abruptly, which can cause the muzzles to dip so that the
       shot goes low.
   2  Do not take the second target for granted, especially in
       a tail wind.

## Station eight
These last two targets are the bane of most newcomers to Skeet, although the good shots do not consider them a problem.

At first sight they seem impossible, and most newcomers find that they are out and gone in a flash. However, practice soon brings them under control.

Most experienced shooters do not really expect to miss any targets once they have finished with station six.

## Station eight: high house
The foot position varies considerably among the top shooters but the one illustrated is a good starting point from which to experiment. The weight should be evenly distributed.

The muzzles are held level with the target window and between six and eight feet to the right of it. A soft focus is held just to the right of the target window (*never* in it!) and, when the shooter is ready for instant reaction, the target is called.

As soon as the target emerges the muzzles must start moving ahead of it. The gunmount must begin at the same time, the intention being to get the gun fully mounted when the target is still about eight yards short of the centre peg. As soon as it is mounted the shot must be fired instantly, the follow-through being almost unavoidable. The target can be shot with no lead at all but it is much safer to give it about a foot. Then, if the swing slows, the target will still have a chance of being hit.

During the first few encounters the target will appear as little less than a blur, but with practice it will be clearly seen earlier and earlier until eventually it will be focused the moment it leaves the house.

## Station eight: low house

This is the last target on the Skeet field and is possibly slightly more difficult than the preceding one because it is usually emerging against a poorish background instead of sky.

Stance is as normal, the foot position as illustrated. The muzzle-hold position is level with the target window and about six feet outside the edge of the house. A soft focus is held just left of the target window.

A very low crouch is the trademark of most of the US ISU Skeet shooters—not a copy-book style, but effective!

It is important that the background is not focused at all.

As with the high target, it is necessary to move the moment this one appears and to stay ahead of it as the gun is being mounted. Again, the intention should be to mount the gun fully when the target is still about eight yards short of the centre peg, then to fire immediately and follow-through .

A lead of about a foot is best, although this one can also be shot dead on.

Note that these two targets are different in one major respect. The high target flies almost level, while the low one climbs quite steeply. Watch for this.

*Possible errors*

1 Trying to make sure of these two will always result in a miss.

2 Only call when absolutely ready.

3 These two are missed if the shooter rushes the gunmount, then stops. There *is* time to shoot these smoothly; it just takes practice and confidence.

4 Once you find a way to break these targets consistently, stick with it, even if it is rather unorthodox!

5 If you have hit all the rest, do not panic, even if you are about to shoot your first twenty-five straight. Concentrate fully and be aggressive with them. Do not try powder-puff tactics on these two!

## Domestic Skeet disciplines

Regardless of the different rules applied to the various Skeet disciplines, all have one thing in common: the Skeet field itself.

It is quite simple, therefore, to transpose the ideas put forward for ISU Skeet and tailor them, without much modification, to suit any of the domestic disciplines. Because these targets are somewhat slower, the recommended hold positions may be modified slightly so that the gun muzzles are brought closer to the respective houses. Many shooters, however, will find even this change unnecessary.

Perhaps surprisingly, the recommended leads will apply equally well to English or NSSA Skeet as they do to ISU, in spite of the difference in target speed, the major factor as regards lead being range rather than the velocity of the targets.

The only aspect which will almost certainly differ is that of the low gun position at address. This is mandatory in ISU Skeet but only a masochist would choose to start in this position when shooting the domestic forms!

To my mind, these domestic disciplines are perfect vehicles for the sustained lead method, the more precision possible with this approach ideally suiting the slower targets. Because the targets *are* slower, it is very easy to shoot every target this way, including the second targets of all doubles (with one notable exception!) Indeed, it is a fair assumption, having watched quite a number of top-class Americans shoot, to say that the majority of them shoot sustained lead and that it certainly helps them shoot the enormous scores for which they are justly renowned.

# Shooting English Skeet

This very popular discipline differs in a number of ways from ISU Skeet, apart from the target speed and address position.

The actual order in which the targets are shot is different, as well as the fact that station eight is not used, and there is no random delay on the target release. The latter factor causes a few problems when a nervous or slow-reacting person is operating the target release button. The English Skeet shooter, like his DTL counterpart, expects the target *NOW* when he calls 'pull', not a split second later (or sometimes longer!) The only answers here are to employ independent and proven referees or to keep the slow-coaches away from the button!

### Ready position
With the ready or address position optional in this form of Skeet it is difficult to judge exactly where to hold the gun prior to calling for the target. In the USA, it is quite normal for the majority of Skeet shooters to assume a ready position with the gun already in the shoulder, Trap style. In Great Britain, however, few shooters concentrate on English Skeet to the exclusion of all else, many of them preferring to include Sporting in their repertoire. This means that a considerable amount of their shooting will require the gun to be out of the shoulder when the target is called, so that trying to shoot 'gun up' at Skeet will feel very stilted and artificial.

Many English Skeet shooters compromise by holding the gun dropped just a few inches down from the shoulder, and it seems a satisfactory solution. It allows the shooter the same freedom of movement afforded by the normal Sporting position, while at the same time making for a simple gunmounting movement. This in itself almost guarantees that the gunmount will be correct and thus one of the principle reasons for missing is practically eliminated.

### Stance
The stance and foot positions as suggested for ISU Skeet will work just as well for the English version. After all, it is only the target speed that is different, not the Skeet field, nor the angle at which the targets fly, nor their range and height.

Because the targets for the discipline are that much slower, however, it is unfortunately possible to shoot good scores while employing the most peculiar stance positions. While this may seem to be acceptable as long as it works, observation of the *top* American Skeet shooters indicates that very few of them stand any way other than fairly erect and in good balance. To my mind, this is the best way to shoot any discipline; no frills.

## Where to look

Because the targets come without any delay after the call, the point is not crucial. The shooter can almost guarantee that as the word 'pull' (or whatever) leaves his mouth the target will be out and on its way. However, looking directly into the target window will still make the target difficult to see in the initial stages of its flight.

As with ISU Skeet, the muzzle elevation at address should be slightly below the anticipated flightline of the target.

## The station four: double

Although I am sure many people will not agree, I have always felt that English Skeet lost a little something when the station eight targets were exchanged for a double on station four. The main objection was that suddenly a none-too-easy double reared its head and removed the possibility of 'robotic shooting', one of the great attractions of the domestic disciplines. Like DTL or American (ATA) Trap, half the fun was that there were no difficult targets to contend with and high scores were always possible for even the non-expert.

Some were more difficult than others, of course, but the station four double changed all that. It was as though someone had decided to throw the occasional ABT target during a round of DTL! Most of the regular English Skeet shooters have come to terms with them now, but they can still be tricky in any sort of wind.

The singles can be taken exactly as the ISU targets. Taking the double brings us on to fresh ground, though. To say 'Shoot it like the double on station three' is not good enough, because this double is not at all like the ISU Skeet double on station three.

One of the few pleasant aspects of the speedy ISU targets is that they hold their line reasonably well in any conditions, whereas the slower English Skeet targets tend to flop a little once they get a few yards past the centre peg. The second target of the station four double suffers from this problem and it can become a very difficult proposition indeed.

The first thing to decide is which of these targets to shoot first. Most right-handers will opt to shoot the high target, since it is the more difficult direction in which to swing. However, it may be more efficient to shoot first whichever target happens to be flying downwind. If this downwind target is shot second, it is a fair bet that it will be almost on the ground by the time the shooter gets to it!

Whichever way you choose to shoot the double, the first target must not be rushed. Shooting it in its usual place over the centre peg is soon enough. This will allow sufficient time to reverse the swing, and catch and swing through the second target.

The second one is quite a long shot and it is tempting to give it a lot more lead than it requires. Always remember that it is slowing down by the time it is shot, so that three to four feet are enough. One of the great points about this second target is that the shooter must really find it with his eyes as soon as he reverses his swing from the first shot. It is too late if the target is only just registered as the muzzles swing past it five feet too high!

*Possible errors*
Lots of possible errors, of course, but below are some of the
more obvious ones.
1  Good balance is of prime importance in any Skeet double
   featuring widely-angled targets. They do not come any
   wider than this one! A stance which allows a fairly
   neutral balance is best, with the weight just slightly
   favouring the forward foot. Avoid falling towards the first
   target as recovery for the second is then very difficult.
2  Do not rush the first shot. Over the centre peg is early
   enough. It is better to hit one than miss two!
3  Do not just slash blindly at the second target; there is time
   to shoot it correctly.
4  If the second target has become a matter for despair,
   check how the *first* target is being shot. The answer could
   be there.

## Shooting high scores

Shooting high Skeet scores is a matter of understanding the
fundamentals of each shot on every station, then applying those
principles in practice and competition. This requires correct thinking.
The fundamentals have already been described, but what about the
thinking? There is an old saying that runs, 'All you think about is the
next target', but there's more to it than that.

The good Skeet shooter plots his way around the Skeet field, rather
like a rock climber scaling a steep face: carefully and methodically,
with no sudden rushes of blood to the head! Also, like the rock climber,
the Skeet shooter knows that there are certain parts of the operation
which are relatively 'safe', whereas others require maximum attention.

The experienced Skeet shooter regards a round of Skeet like this:
some targets are near certainties or 'bankers': no one expects to miss
them. Others are a little more difficult, while a few of them are
positively tricky.

To clarify this we will go through a round of English Skeet, rating
each target on a scale of 1-4, with 4 being the most difficult.

| **Station one** | **Rating** |
|---|---|
| high house single | 2 |
| low house single | 1 |
| double, high & low | 2 & 1 |
| **Station two** | |
| high single | 4 |
| low house single | 1 |
| double, high & low | 4 & 2 |

**Station three**

| | |
|---|---|
| high single | 4 |
| low single | 3 |

**Station four**

| | |
|---|---|
| both singles | 3 |
| double, first & second target | 3 & 4 |

**Station five**

| | |
|---|---|
| high single | 3 |
| low single | 4 |

**Station six**

| | |
|---|---|
| high single | 1 |
| low single | 3 |
| double, low & high | 3 & 2 |

**Station seven**

| | |
|---|---|
| high single | 1 |
| low single | 2 |
| double, low & high | 2 & 1 |

Whilst not everybody will agree with these particular ratings, the principle can be readily understood. Targets rated '1 & 2' ought never to be missed. This adds up to twelve targets. Targets rated '3' are more difficult and will occasionally get away from even the best shooters. However, they again ought not to be missed. The targets rated '4' are not difficult by normal shooting standards and a good Sporting shot would expect to break them most of the time.

This, of course, is the rub; at Skeet, 'most of the time' is not good enough. The winning Skeet shooter must break them *all* of the time, and the targets rated '4' are sufficiently awkward to make it difficult to achieve.

Luckily (by my rating system, anyway), there are but six such targets to contend with in a round of Skeet and the wise Skeet shooter will give these his very keenest attention.

It can be seen, therefore, that scores in the 80% area are well within the reach of anyone who spends a little time and effort learning the basics, and that it is quite possible for someone lacking great shooting talent to score very respectably at any of the Skeet disciplines, the ISU version included.

# 8
## Trap Shooting

Of all the various clay shooting disciplines, Trapshooting of one sort or another is undoubtedly the oldest form, pre-dating Skeet by at least fifty years. It was devised as a replacement for what was then the recently outlawed sport of live pigeon shooting and has flourished ever since.

There are a number of Trapshooting disiplines to choose from, with the ubiquitous 'Down the Line' being the most popular and least expensive to set up. Its fixed height, varied-angle single trap also makes for easy installation, as well as making a portable layout a distinct possibility. Contrast this with the requirements of an Olympic layout (as described in the next chapter) and one of the main reasons for the popularity of DTL becomes immediately apparent.

Olympic Trap, as the name suggests, is the form of Trapshooting featured in the Olympic Games and is probably the most demanding of all the Trap disciplines. Unfortunately, it is also far and away the most expensive to install, requiring fifteen traps per layout, a computer-controlled acoustic target-release system, plus a pretty hefty investment in structural and excavation work.

In between these two extremes are several other similar disciplines, all of which share one feature in common with these two examples: all the targets fly away from the shooter, either straight or at an angle.

## Down the Line

DTL, the most mild of all the trap disciplines, has five shooting stations positioned in an arc sixteen yards behind the trap. The targets, which are relatively slow, are of fixed elevation yet they are varied unpredictably through fixed angles to the left and right. With two shots allowed at each target, 100 straights are fairly commonplace so points are awarded according to whether the target is broken with the first or the second shot. A first shot counts three, a second counts two, so that at the end of the competition it is the shooter with the most points who wins, not necessarily the one with the most hits.

There are a number of variations of DTL which are also keenly shot.

### Single barrel
Single barrel DTL is the same as the US ATA Trapshooting where only one shot per target is allowed. To many people this makes a lot

more sense than the current DTL rules, which permit two shots. However, DTL is very much the preserve of the traditionalists and the chances of the rules being changed are rather slim.

### Handicap

Handicap trap is another interesting Trap game, the shooter being handicapped according to his skill level by having to stand at a greater distance from the trap house than usual. In Great Britain the maximum handicap distance is twenty-three yards, whereas in the USA, where this game is much more regularly shot, the full handicap distance is twenty-seven yards. As anyone who has shot the discipline will testify, Trapshooting takes on a whole new perspective with targets starting this far away! However, despite the fact that the targets look extremely small when shot at such a range, some shooters still manage to shoot the lot.

For those who may be concerned, 27 yd Trap shooters never shoot in the same squad as those who must stand much closer!

### Double rise

This is another variation on DTL, this time with two targets being thrown simultaneously instead of one. The extreme angle targets in these doubles are considerably wider than those of DTL, too, so high scoring is difficult. Again, as with handicap Trap, this form is much more popular in the USA than it is in Britain.

### Back-up Trap

I have never heard of anyone shooting this in the UK, but it is quite popular in the USA. Two shooters share each station, the idea being that one of the two is the shooter while the other is his back-up man.

Theoretically, at least, the shooter fires at each target which, if he misses, is then shot at by the back-up man. For the back-up man to be effective, it is necessary that he tracks the target at the same time as the shooter. If he fires before the shooter he suffers a penalty but, as can be imagined, chaos soon reigns! Having been involved in this mayhem I can recommend that it is not introduced in Britain!

## Automatic Ball Trap

Most shooters, many of whom have little regard for the sensibilities of the average layman, call this simply 'Ball Trap', a title guaranteed to cause raised eyebrows in any group as well as looks of disbelief. The more thoughtful shooters tend to refer to it as ABT when in mixed company, while the Americans refer to it as 'Wobble Trap', itself quite evocative, or, least offensive of all, simply as 'Continental'.

One of its great attractions is that it is very similar in some ways to Olympic Trap, throwing as it does targets which not only vary their angles more widely than DTL, but also vary their height. In addition, they are a good deal faster than DTL, too.

There have been a number of attempts in the last few years to make ABT the official discipline for the Olympic Games, the idea being that as it is considerably cheaper to instal and run than an equivalent Olympic layout, participation by a far greater number of countries and shooters would be possible. Retaining as it does many of the features of Olympic Trap, this might be thought to be a reasonable assumption, but more of that later.

## Olympic Trap

Olympic Trap is the most challenging of all the trap disciplines, as well as being one of the fairest. An on-site computer ensures that each shooter gets exactly the same distribution of target angles, heights, and speeds in every round of twenty-five, although not, of course, in the same sequence. How this is effected is described in detail in the next chapter.

It is this element of fairness that is the significant difference between O/T and ABT for, unlike the former, ABT is entirely random in its target distribution. It can mean that in a given squad one shooter has all the steadily rising and easy angle targets, while another seems to draw all the more difficult lower and wider ones.

The impartiality of O/T probably guarantees that it will never be replaced by ABT, in spite of the development of a computerised system that will allow the ABT trap to throw random/repeat targets. However, last estimates indicated that such a system would equal or exceed that of an Olympic layout in cost, yet would still leave O/T with an ace in the hole: varying target speed.

Within an O/T 'scheme' the targets are set so that some are fast, some are very fast and some are (relatively!) slow, and this is a factor that no ABT system can ever duplicate, computer or no computer.

## Universal Trench

Something of a bastard version of Olympic Trap, U/T is not an ISU discipline (though no worse for that), but one controlled by FITASC. It does not really have the following of O/T, probably because many of the layouts that throw U/T targets are slightly modified O/T fields, it being possible, with slight modifications here and there, to pop back and forth between the two as simply as you can with ISU Skeet and English Skeet. So why shoot Universal when the same layout will throw the more sophisticated Olympic targets?

Universal Trench utilises five fixed line traps instead of the fifteen of O/T.

Where an O/T layout is used in modified form, the five middle traps of the bank of fifteen are adjusted as necessary. The rightmost trap throws the widest target to the left, the leftmost does the opposite, the two inside these throw similar but reduced angle targets, while the centre throws relatively straight ones. However, owing to the fact that the shooters move around these fixed traps, the angles vary considerably.

The reason the leftmost trap of both U/T and O/T throws its target to the right and not, as might be thought, to the left and *vice versa*, is so that the targets are seen by the shooters to leave the trap house from almost exactly the same position, thus enabling a relatively consistent 'hold' position to be maintained from shot to shot. Why make it easier in this way? Most people think it and O/T are quite hard enough already!

## Shooting 'Down the Line'

Trap shooters are rather fortunate in that they have so many disciplines from which to choose and this, particularly for the beginner, is very important.

DTL has a number of attractions: not only is it sufficiently interesting in its own right to keep experienced shooters coming back for more, it also provides an excellent training ground for those who arc aspiring international-style shooters.

One of its great advantages for the neophyte is that the relatively slow targets do not cause the shooter panic, a very important point when one is striving to make the best of untrained reflexes. As such, it is the ideal way to acquire good Trapshooting form without simultaneously being pressured into attempting to catch rapidly dwindling international-style targets! An introduction to Trapshooting on any of these faster Trap disciplines is the sort of baptism by fire which deters many potential shooters.

One of the features of DTL which is slightly controversial is the permitted use of two barrels per target whenever necessary, scoring 3 points for a first barrel 'kill' and 2 for a second. While this may seem like overkill on such targets, there can be little doubt that for budding internationals it is an excellent way of learning to use the second barrel. (All international Trap disciplines permit the full use of the gun, kills to count.)

One of the criticisms sometimes aimed at DTL is that it is too easy and the scores are too high. While there can be no denying that, target for target, DTL is arguably easier than, say, ABT, it does not make it any easier to actually win! The whole point of disciplines such as DTL (English Skeet is another which comes to mind) is that they allow relatively inexperienced shooters to go home having broken a respectable score, whilst at the same time they still offer sufficient challenge to those people who wish to devote more time and effort to breaking the lot.

The ultimate challenge of DTL, however, as with all the other disciplines, is not just to break 100 targets first barrel only (although no one will turn their nose up at this!), but to win the competition.

# The DTL Layout

The illustration is easy enough to understand. As can be seen, the extreme right-hand target goes straight away from station one, while the extreme left-hand one goes directly away from station five. With such clearcut definitions of exactly what constitutes a good target or a 'no bird', it is little wonder that so much trouble is caused when a shooter claims that his target was too wide, especially when the referee is a fellow-shooter in the same competition. Hopefully, something along American lines will eventually be adopted: if you shoot at it you are deemed to have accepted it as a valid target, so that if you subsequently miss said target, hard luck. It is gone!

The official distance the target must fly is between 50 and 55 yards. Although an ideal distance of 52 yards is recommended, it is highly unlikely that any trap, automatic or otherwise, will be found capable of throwing targets accurately enough so that all of them fall at this exact distance. Most people will be happy if the targets remain within the specified 50-55 yards area.

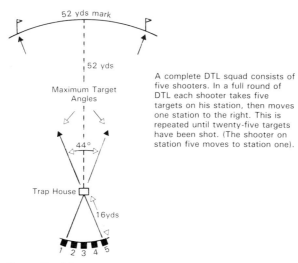

A complete DTL squad consists of five shooters. In a full round of DTL each shooter takes five targets on his station, then moves one station to the right. This is repeated until twenty-five targets have been shot. (The shooter on station five moves to station one).

Layout for Down-the-Line.

At a distance 10 yards from the trap the target must clear a height of 8 feet and be no higher at this distance than 10. It can easily be set with the aid of a T-pole or a raised hoop, Skeet-style. These measurements must be adhered to quite rigidly, of course, or else everyone is thrown by the discrepancy, the experienced shots probably more so than the beginners.

The trap is ideally an auto-angling device which has an unreadable and random target spread, thus ensuring that nobody knows what is coming out next. The original auto varying traps were only too readable, since they swung regularly left to right/right to left in a very predictable fashion, making the game a little easy for those who could anticipate the trap's movements.

Target release is another bone of contention amongst regular shooters. The target is supposed to come the instant the shooter calls for it and one of the most aggravating things when shooting Trap is to have someone in charge of the target release button who has either poor reflexes or is very nervous! When someone like this is in charge anything can happen and usually does. Fast pulls, slow pulls, and even no pulls are all possible and eventually, of course, targets will be missed and words will be exchanged.

To follow the route of the majority of international disciplines and have targets released electronically is a possible, but hardly cheap, alternative. The only reasonable approach is to have independent 'pullers' who at least cannot be accused by shooters of having a vested interest in the results.

Whatever may be said about DTL, it has a larger number of adherents both at home and abroad, albeit in slightly modified form, and this alone speaks volumes. Add to that the extremely uncomplicated rules and high-scoring possibilities and you have a discipline which has been around many years and will continue to be around for many more, too.

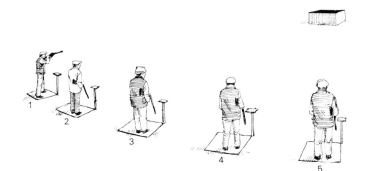

Squad shooting Down-the-Line.

## Learning DTL

One of the initial difficulties experienced by newcomers to Trap, particularly those who have spent a lot of time shooting Sporting or Skeet, or maybe have previously shot just game, is that caused by the Trapshooting 'address' position, which involves starting with the gun fully mounted. While this may seem a boon to the absolute beginner, it can prove very awkward for everyone else. (A detailed description of DTL technique is printed on pages 115-120.)

For the experienced non-Trap man, one of the most disorientating things about the 'gun-up' position is the fact that the barrels and rib suddenly become very attractive to the eye, because if ever a shooting game seems to lend itself to a bit of rifle-style aiming, Trap is it! Needless to say, this is not to be recommended. However easy certain Trap targets may appear to be, they still require all the technique and skill applicable to other forms of shotgun shooting if the result is to be successful. In fact, strange though it may seem, the most frequently missed targets in all forms of Trapshooting are the straight away shots.

In the early stages, many experienced shooters who are unfamiliar with Trap find that it is actually more productive to start with the gun out of the shoulder, mounting it, as in other forms of shooting, as the target appears. Certainly, as far as instant results are concerned, this will get some of the targets broken but it is hardly likely to prove a reliable system if high scores are anticipated.

## Preparing to shoot

Setting up correctly prior to calling for a target is as important when shooting DTL as it is for any of the other clay disciplines. As in the case of Skeet or Sporting, what is ideal is a method which the shooter can adopt automatically every time he sets up to take a shot. Although such a method may well take some time to absorb, the shooter will eventually be able to allow his mind to concentrate on just one thing: the target.

While it must be accepted that nothing can ever make up for a lack of talent, careful attention to detail can go a long way towards redressing the balance between the gifted and those not so fortunate.

## The gunmount

One point which must be made at the outset is that the gunmount *position* as used for Trap is exactly the same as that used for any other form of shotgun shooting, whether it happens to be Skeet, Sporting or whatever. Although for Trap the gun starts ready-mounted, the actual position in the shoulder and face should be the same as that for the other disciplines.

Referring back to the earlier comment about rifle shooting, it is very easy for the Trapshooter to mount the gun in such a way as to necessitate a forcing down of the face onto the stock, thus creating unwanted tension in the neck and shoulders. This can lead to a number of problems.

Tension in these areas makes any movement stiff and awkward, and eventually it can easily spread through the arms and body until the shooter is unable to swing smoothly at all. Also, following the first shot, it is all too easy for the face to come off the stock into a more natural head-up position and this will amost certainly mean that the second shot will be wasted.

Many Trapshooters get around the problem by deliberately making a gunmount with the muzzles pointing well above the trap house, which makes it much easier to keep the head in the correct position as the gun is being mounted. Thus correctly positioned, the shooter then lowers the muzzles to the correct address position relative to the traphouse, being careful as he does so not to alter the established relationship between himself and the gun.

To the beginner, this established position may look as though the shooter's head has dropped and that his face has pushed down hard on the stock, but it is an illusion. The correct position is one that the newcomer should try to learn at the very beginning of his Trapshooting career.

Establishing the actual eye-rib relationship at address is the next important point. Some shooters like their eye to be flat along the rib while others prefer to be looking slightly over it. There are pros and cons for both ways. With the eye flat along the rib at address the shooter is absolutely certain that his eye-rib relationship is always exactly the same, and this is very important if consistency is to be achieved. However, on the debit side, such a position means two things:

1 If the shooter can see the target as he shoots, he must be pointing below the target to do so, however slightly, perhaps not the best thing on a target which is rising.

2 On the other hand, for the gun to be centring on the target, the shooter must 'blot it out' with the barrels just as he shoots. While this is something which only occurs for a fraction of a second, it still means that at the optimum moment when the shot is being fired, the target is not seen.

For those who prefer to see the target all the time the problem is simple: how high above the rib must the eye be set and how do you keep it there? The simple answer to the second question is, 'With plenty of practice!'

The first question is not quite so straightforward. An old method for establishing the eye-rib relationship (and just as valid now) is to place a ten pence piece on the end of the rib nearest the eye. When the entire bead at the muzzle end can be just seen over the coin, the eye-rib relationship is about right. When this is done and the coin removed, the rib appears to be pointing slightly up, and this compensates for the rising DTL target. It also means the target can be seen throughout the shot.

Some Trap gun manufacturers include a mid-bead which, as the name suggests, is a bead that sits on the rib halfway between the front bead and the breech. The purpose of the smaller bead is the same as that served by the coin except, of course, that the bead is a feature of the gun. The shooter knows that his eye-rib relationship is correct when he can just see the front bead perched on top of the mid-bead, 'figure eighting' as the Americans call it.

Some shooters find the presence of these extra beads a distraction, while others love them. One good thing for those who do not like them is that they can easily be unscrewed and removed, to be refitted if the day ever comes when the gun has to be sold.

Whether you choose to shoot with the eye flat along the rib or slightly raised is something with which to experiment. The vast majority of DTL shooters prefer the latter, although there is not such an overwhelming preference for this eye position in the other Trap disciplines. More of that later.

The other important point related to this eye positioning is the actual gun fit itself. Most trap guns these days come with stocks that are either high or very high, and with the latter it can be sometimes impossible to set up for the correct eye position without some forcing down of the head being necessary. This is obviously undesirable and serves to underline the importance of a well-fitted gun. Sorting it out is to be considered a priority. (See Gun Fit on page 38.)

# DTL Technique

## Stance
I have seen two quite different stances used successfully over the years by famous shooters in the UK.

One could be described as the classical stance of the game shot, while the other involves the shooter standing with his chest more squarely facing the traphouse. What follows is a detailed description of each, with examples of noteworthy practitioners.

### The classical stance
Using the face of a clock as a means of orientation, the stance is as follows.

The line from the shooter to the traphouse represents twelve o'clock on the clock face. The shooter's left foot points towards a position between one and two o'clock and his right foot points towards three o'clock. A line drawn across the tips of the shooter's toes would point towards eleven o'clock.

The shooter's weight favours the left foot and the right heel, whilst in contact with the ground, is at the point of leaving it should any more weight be transferred to the left side. Indeed, during the act of shooting the target, more weight *is* transferred to the left side and the right heel very definitely leaves the ground. The cause of this transference of weight is quite simply that it is brought about by the shooter pushing himself and the muzzles of the gun at the target as it leaves the traphouse.

On anything other than a straight away target this raising of the heel has a particularly beneficial effect. It permits the whole body to rotate with the gun in a horizontal plane about its pivot point, the left leg. In addition, the transference of weight in such a fashion helps to stabilise the shooter against the effects of recoil, as well as making the shot a more aggressive attack on the target, something which is lacking in a passive and upright stance.

Famous competitors in Great Britain who adopted this stance and approach include Percy Stanbury, Joe Wheater and Brian Bailey.

### The trapshooter's stance
The distinction between this stance and the one just described is as follows.

The classical stance is one which has been *adapted* to suit Trapshooting, whereas the Trapshooter's stance is one more commonly seen amongst those who shoot Trap almost exclusively. As stated earlier, it involves the shooter standing more square-on to the traphouse. In doing so, the left foot points towards twelve o'clock (towards the traphouse), and the right foot points towards two o'clock.

To my mind, this is an unnatural position which has a tendency to make the shooter swing the gun with just his arms instead of his whole body. This, of course, can result in the head coming away from the stock, with disastrous results to the outcome of the shot.

Those who are devotees of the stance compensate for this deficiency in the method by bending the knees so that they are able to turn to angled targets. They do, therefore, effect a solution to the problem of the gun leaving the face, but it seems to me to be a good example of one of the rare times when two 'wrongs' can make something approximating a 'right'!

I cannot help thinking that whilst excellent scores are often recorded by those who use this stance, it is in spite of the method, rather than because of it.

## Hold positions

The following is a description of the various gunpoint options open to the DTL shooter when setting up in preparation to shoot.

### Muzzle height at address

Like the stances, there are two quite separate schools of thought as to how high the gun should be pointed relative to the traphouse prior to calling for the target.

One method is to hold the muzzles so that they point above the traphouse roofline and the other is to hold them so that they point on or below this line. It is not proposed to say which of these is correct as it is essentially a matter of personal preference, and there are sound arguments in support of both methods.

Some maintain that it is better to have the gun held low so that the target is immediately visible when it appears. Others say that since the targets are rising it is advantageous to start with the muzzles higher so that less movement is required to catch it.

The latter method does have a drawback in that a straight away target is temporarily obscured by the muzzles. There are ways round this involving guns with special top rib configurations, but these are beyond the scope of the chapter. Anyone who is sufficiently bothered by the problem of the obscured target would be well advised to experiment with a lower hold position before being lured into purchasing expensive exotica.

### Lateral muzzle position at address

As with muzzle height, there are two schools of thought as to the lateral placement of the muzzle relative to the traphouse roof.

One school maintains that the shooter should always point the gun at the top centre of the roof regardless of the station on which he happens to be shooting. The other says that the traphouse roofline should be split up into sections so that on the extreme ends of the layout, pegs one and five, the muzzles should be positioned on the nearest front corner of the traphouse to steal a march on any extreme angle target which may emerge.

Both these ideas have their pros and cons, and it is my experience that more straight or nearly straight targets are missed at trap than are angled ones.

The first system mentioned ensures that on the extremities of the layout the muzzles are always directly in line with an emerging straight target. The shooter has only to raise his barrels to the target and shoot as soon as the elevation is correct.

With the second system the shooter not only has to raise the muzzles to achieve the correct elevation, he also has to bring the muzzles across to the correct line. This is no easy thing to do faultlessly, particularly if the shooter's natural timing is relatively fast.

The 'centre pointer' does admittedly have more catching up to do whenever he draws an acutely-angled target on pegs one or five but the only consequence of this is that he shoots these targets a yard or two later than does his 'intercepting' counterpart.

For what it's worth, I have tried all methods and found that they work reasonably well, but on average I have done better using the 'centre point' method.

## Where to look

There can be no argument on this point. You must look over the barrels into the space where you will first be able to pick up the target as it emerges from the traphouse. When looking out for the target it is important to allow the eyes to take a soft focus, which means not letting the eyes focus on anything in particular.

The shooter should be extremely alert and should try to experience a sort of flash of concentrated effort at the moment of calling for the target, almost like throwing the switch to turn on an electric light. Your first concern will be establishing that the target has indeed come out! Your second will be to note its direction laterally. Hence, where you look relative to the top of the traphouse is governed by these considerations.

It is obviously foolish to look for the target against a background which renders it all but invisible. This may mean having to look higher than would normally be ideal so that the target can be clearly seen. It would not, for example, be much use expecting to see a black target against a background of burnt heather or grass. All layouts have backgrounds peculiar to themselves and all that one can hope for is that the ground owners have been sensible in their choice of location.

## Training

When one has developed the competence to hit twenty or so targets out of twenty-five, it is time to start analysing the reasons why.

Ry this stage, it probably comes down to insufficient concentration on each shot. Most times, the mind has wandered between shots and some defence mechanism has to be found which will prevent this happening.

As an aid to concentration I used to pick a spot on the traphouse, such as a rivet mark, and stare at it the whole time I was on the line, except when I had to close the gun and shoot my target. I did not take my eyes off it even to load my gun! Changing stations was the only time I allowed myself a respite.

I am not suggesting that everyone has to follow my lead, but it was a simple method that I used to avoid the intrusion of extraneous thoughts and distractions. Others find that lowering their eyes and looking at the ground serves the same purpose.

I have only seen one really top shooter who did not employ some consistent ploy to keep his mind on the job in hand and that was Brian Bailey. Brian would look everywhere, wink at the crowd, grin and yet still hit his 100 straights! I don't know how he got away with it and perhaps he would have been even greater at DTL if he had been more insular. On the other hand, perhaps his actual flamboyance served as his inspiration in the same way as it did for that great golfer, the late Walter Hagen. He maintained that, regardless of the seriousness of the situation, one should always find time to 'stop and smell the flowers'. Perhaps he had a point.

### Who to shoot with?

Sorting out the shooters that you can and cannot get on with is a matter of some importance. It probably comes down to deciding not so much who to shoot with but, more relevantly, who must be avoided!

It is distracting to shoot with someone who is erratic in their timing. This shooter will use varying amounts of time to take each shot which, in turn, throws the rhythm of the entire squad. It can turn the person in charge of the target-release button into a nervous wreck, too. Nor does it aid the concentration to be constantly hit by the ejected cartridge cases of your next door neighbour's automatic.

Where possible, it is best to shoot in a regular five-man squad where everyone gets along and each shooter knows what to expect from the others.

### Which station to start on?

Everyone has his own preference, and I used to like to shoot in the number one position most of all. In this way I felt I could dictate the pace of the squad and make sure everything happened in an orderly fashion.

Some people like to start on station three, the middle, so that they do not have to face any extreme-angle targets until they have fired a few shots and 'got their eye in'.

Brian Bailey always shot first on station four, given the chance. He reasoned that station four targets were hardly any more difficult than

Squad of five shoot Down-the-Line.

Even the worst weather does not deter keen Down-the-Line shooters! Note the acoustic release microphones.

those from station three and if he was in contention at the end of the day he would then be finishing on station three and have an easier time of it as the pressure increased.

### Ammunition

I do not believe that any sort of special ammunition is required to shoot DTL as long as the shot size used is no. 7 or 8.

Some people like to shoot no. 8s in the first barrel and no. 7s in the second on the basis that the 8s give a better close-range pattern density, while the 7s are more effective at the longer ranges.

I always feel that this is a waste of time, for at the sort of distances at which the typical DTL shooter takes his targets, even with the second barrel, 7s or 8s will do the job equally well. If, on the other hand, a shooter is spectacularly slow then it probably will not make much difference what he shoots with, anyway!

## In conclusion

So there we are. As with all the other disciplines, it would be quite possible to fill an encyclopedia with DTL know-how but this will have to do for now. DTL is probably one of the few clay shooting disciplines which can truly be all things to all men, certainly more so than English Skeet with all its attendant equipment, and arguably more than the somewhat undisciplined English Sporting!

It can be an enjoyable ten target bangabout for the lads at the local fete; a semi-serious game at the local Sunday shoot; an excellent training discipline for aspiring internationals but, and most importantly of all, a testing enough Trap game to have inspired very large numbers of intelligent shooters through the years into attempting to achieve a degree of mastery over it. Few have succeeded.

# 9

# Olympic
# Trap

Olympic Trap has often been described as the 'Formula One' of clay target shooting. While I am not certain that it is an accurate assessment, there can be little doubt that, shot for shot, Olympic Trap is overall the most expensive form of clay shooting and is arguably the most popular from an international standpoint. This is thanks in no small part to the Italians who have some one and a half *million* registered clay target shooters, the majority of whom shoot Olympic Trap to the exclusion of all else.

With a home market as healthy as this it is little wonder that much of the serious clay-shooting hardware comes from Italy, nor is it surprising that Italian shooters regularly feature in the medal lists at all levels of international competition.

Exactly why Olympic Trap is such an attractive clay-shooting discipline is hard to define. The targets are fast and elusive, and the worthwhile ammunition is expensive, as are the initial layout installation costs. Nevertheless, it has a certain air of 'class' about it which is perhaps lacking in some of the other clay disciplines and possibly this factor alone is what lures some shooters into giving it a try.

For the dyed-in-the-wool DTL shooter Olympic Trap can come as something of a shock. The vast majority of layouts have computer-controlled acoustic target release, which means that the target is off the trap arm and going rapidly on its way almost before the call of 'pull' has left the shooter's lips. For the shooter used to a slight reaction delay on the part of the button boy or referee this can be somewhat distracting.

The targets themselves are not only a good deal faster than those of DTL, they also vary in speed from trap to trap. Although this variation is only a matter of several yards over the full thrown distance between one target and another, it is, nevertheless, significant. A low widely-angled target travelling the maximum permitted distance is a very different proposition to one gliding a few yards shorter but on a higher trajectory. All these speed variations are laid down within the 'scheme' system and so cannot be altered at the whim of the shoot organisers.

In DTL, each shooter fires at five targets from the station on which he starts his round before moving one station to his right, the man on station five moving round to station one. With this system each squad consists of five shooters. In Olympic Trap, and in all the international Trap disciplines for that matter, there are six men per squad although there are still only five stations.

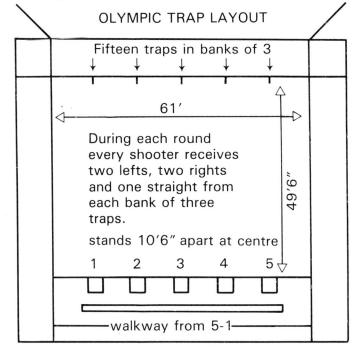

Layout for Olympic Trap.

What happens at the beginning of the round is as follows. Shooters 1-5 go to their respective stations while number 6 stands behind and out of sight of number 1. Number 1 shoots and then waits: number 2 takes his shot, after which number 1 walks to station two and stands beside the man who has just shot. Number 6 now occupies station one. When number 3 has shot, number 2 walks up to him, and number 1 then occupies station two, and so on. It is much easier done than described! This constant moving up and down can be rather confusing at first, and it is very easy to lose count of how many targets have been shot. A quick glance at the scoreboard will soon solve the problem of course.

Olympic Trap is unique in the sense that, unlike all the other Trap disciplines, the shooter never moves around the trap or traps at which he will be shooting: the ones with which he will be concerned are always in front of him. The total number of fifteen fixed-line traps are set up to conform with any one of the nine different 'schemes' and, theoretically, each bank of three traps should be installed in such a way that regardless of whether they throw left, right or straight targets these emerge from the same point in front of the shooter.

It is very important that the installation be exactly right because the shooter shapes much of his style and technique around this very factor. In any discipline as demanding as this, apparently small changes can have a dramatic effect on the form of the shooters affected. From the viewpoint of shooting technique the same thing applies.

The discipline allows two shots per target, breaking the target with either counting as one point. Unlike DTL, where one shot/one target would bring a breath of fresh air to the discipline, Olympic Trap would become a very low-scoring game indeed if the shooters were to be limited in the same way. A very rare sight even at international events is an OT '25 straight' achieved without recourse to the second barrel.

One gets the feeling that Olympic Trap shooters, even when shooting well, are always just a hair's breadth away from disaster and this is borne out by results. Few shooters seem to sustain a high scoring average for long.

One reason for this is that, in common with Universal Trench, there is no possibility of the shooter getting an 'easy ride' on any particular round: everyone shoots exactly the same variation of targets although in a different sequence. In DTL and the faster ABT, with unreadable and auto-varying traps, it is possible for one shooter to receive all easy angle targets and for another to get all the harder ones. In Skeet the shooter knows where he must concentrate extra hard and also where he can perhaps throttle back a bit. The Sporting shooter will have easy stands, and some less easy. The OT shooter, however, knows that he will have no easy targets and that every one of them demands 100% concentration.

In a sport which relies so heavily on conditioned reflexes, rather than the careful plotting and planning of the rifle shooter, objective advice on technique is difficult to come by. In any reflex-based sport, such as clay shooting, what the performer does and what he *thinks* he does are often two entirely different things. This is especially true of Olympic Trap.

Having observed a large number of top OT shooters and then spoken to them regarding technique, it is apparent that for many of them their technique is something which has only evolved as a result of a great deal of OT shooting. For these shooters, technique exists almost entirely in the subconscious which, although ultimately the best place for it, usually means that the shooter is unable to self-analyse if something goes wrong. Unfortunately, for the would-be OT shooter, it also means that information from such shooters regarding valid technique for Olympic Trap is rather hard to come by.

The following is therefore a compilation of the techniques observed to be used by many of the top OT shooters from around the world, rather than those of any particular shooter or style.

## Shooting Olympic Trap

To be truly competitive at OT it is obviously essential that the equipment and ammunition be of indisputable quality. Any 'saving' here will be guaranteed to cost a target or targets and the cash value of these is hard to assess. However, having said that it would be foolish for the OT beginner to waste good money on the very best ammunition when the prime cause of his lost targets is his own inexperience. Therefore, it would be wise in the early stages to use something a little less expensive which will certainly do the job without breaking the bank.

Although gun types for the discipline are discussed elsewhere, it should be remembered before moving on that a gun well suited to DTL will not necessarily transport well to the international games. (See Guns on page 24.)

**Stance**

The majority of Olympic Trap shooters favour a narrow stance, some with the feet together and almost touching, while others go in for much wider foot positions, usually in combination with considerable bending at the knees.

Both of these foot positions have certain advantages and disadvantages. The very narrow stance allows great freedom of movement but is somewhat insecure from the viewpoint of balance, particularly in conditions of strong wind. The much wider stance gives good balance but is very restricting unless the knees are well bent. While this is acceptable, it requires the shooter to be pretty fit since the style puts heavy demands on the knee-joints and thigh muscles. While the success of some shooters using this stance is undeniable, it would be difficult to recommend such a position.

Probably the best solution is to experiment with as narrow a stance as possible consistent with good balance, keeping the body relatively erect. This will almost certainly be somewhat narrower than the stance adopted by the typical Skeet shooter, who has to change swing direction completely when shooting doubles. The Trapshooter, on the other hand, commits his balance as his target emerges and does not have to alter it.

**Foot position**

In common with all shotgun shooting games, good Trapshooting is impossible if the shooter cannot turn freely in any direction as required. While a shooter's stance may be perfect, his freedom of movement is governed by how this stance is aligned with the traps.

As in Skeet, standing very square with the toes almost parallel to the front of the station makes turning 'against the gun' very difficult (any shot to the right for a right-handed shooter). A very noticeable binding of the swing occurs, particularly on wide, low right targets, and this has to be compensated for by unwanted twists and heaves.

Standing with the toes parallel to the sides of the station, on the other hand, is likely to make the shooter's whole body align in the same way and this will make gunmounting awkward since the body has to be twisted in order to be properly square with the gun.

The majority of top OT shooters adopt a half-facing position, with their feet aligned as shown in the illustration opposite. This gives the freedom to move in both directions as well as assuring that the body's position is just right for the gunmount.

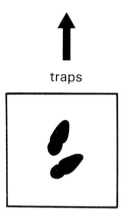

traps

Foot position for Olympic Trap.

Top Great Britain shooter, Peter Croft, takes a sharp-angled Olympic Trap target. Note the narrow stance.

## Gunmounting

In all the Trap disciplines the gun is mounted before the target is called. While there is plenty of time to get the gun mounted exactly right, top shooters vary considerably in the time they take between commencement of the gunmount and the calling of the target. Some take the maximum permitted fifteen seconds while others mount the gun and call almost before the pieces of target of the previous shooter have hit the ground!

One thing is certain though: regardless of how long each individual shooter takes over setting himself up physically and mentally, the actual time taken is always exactly the same. This is meant quite literally. From the moment the shooter to his left has shot, any top

OT shooter will take the same time to the split second to mount the gun, come into his 'hold' position and call for the target. Should there be some slight distraction the shooter will invariably stop and go through the routine again from scratch, thus preserving the feel of the whole shot from start to finish.

The gunmount position should be no different from that used in Sporting or Skeet. However, with targets like these emerging at ground level it is easy when setting up to get into a very crouched head-down position which, apart from being uncomfortable, makes eye-gun-target alignment difficult and a good swing impossible. As this is obviously something to avoid, many OT shooters first mount the gun so that it is pointing somewhat above parallel with the ground. Having thus mounted the gun well, they then lean forward slightly so that the muzzles are lowered to the desired 'hold' position. For these shooters it is an important part of their set-up routine and it never varies.

The other way, equally in favour, is to lean slightly forward first and then to mount the gun directly into the hold position. While a good gunmount with the latter method is more difficult to achieve for the newcomer, it has the great advantage of being more spontaneous with less chance of inducing a deliberate aim down the rib.

The eye-rib relationship is largely governed by the way the gun fits the individual shooter. (See Gun Fit on page 40.) However, for those who have not had their gun adjusted to suit them, it is important that the eye is always positioned slightly above the rib rather than flat along it. While the latter would suit the lowest targets, it would make life difficult on those more steeply-rising. A compromise is therefore in order. For most people the coin trick will do the job, as described on page 114. Ideally, of course, the gun should be fitted in such a way that this eye-rib relationship occurs automatically.

**The hold position**
There are two schools of thought on where the gun should point prior to calling for the target. One says that the gun should point at the target exit position. The other favours holding the gun anything up to several feet above this point.

In the first method the muzzles are exactly on the flightline of the target as it emerges: all the shooter has to do is see the target and move the gun after it. Granted superb reflexes, this works very well. Most normal human beings, unfortunately, do not react quite quick enough and the frequent result of starting the gun in this position is that the shooter is left way behind by the speeding target. Regardless of the type of shotgun shooting under discussion, when the target and the gun become out of touch with one another like this the chances of success are minimal.

What tends to happen is that the shooter moves his head slightly from the stock in order to see the target and, in so doing, destroys the vital relationship between the eye and the gun. The resulting swing relies on the gun being moved very quickly if the rapidly receding target is to be caught, and this makes good timing almost impossible.

Holding the muzzles higher than the target exit point helps overcome these problems. Also, because the shooter is then looking out over a much broader area, he is less inclined to allow his eyes to focus on the ground in front of him. Most shooters find that they are able to move more freely when in this high hold position and, although OT targets are never easy to catch, they are made that little bit easier.

Care has to be exercised when using the position: low targets can very easily slip out under the barrels and be a long way down the range before the shooter picks them up. While this is not too much of a problem with the angled targets, it is a distinct danger when a low straight one zips away! However, if a quick check is carried out at any of the world's major competitions, the majority of OT shooters will be seen to be using a high hold position.

Exactly how high the muzzles should be is a matter for individual experiment. However, if pointing straight at the target exit point is too low for most shooters, then pointing the muzzles in such a way that the barrels are parallel to the ground is too far the other way!

The height of the hold position must sometimes be altered if the background is particularly awkward, although how and when is something the shooter will only learn from experience.

**Where to look**
In any of the Trap disciplines a great temptation for the beginner is to look at the barrels as the target is called. A quick check that everything is properly aligned is acceptable but then the eyes must look out *over* the gun, not at it. As in all forms of shooting, a soft focus should be held in the general area where the target will be emerging. In Olympic Trap, with its wide variation of target angles, this general area is quite large. Focusing on a particular spot on the ground or a tree in the distance can mean the target slipping out without the shooter realising until it is too late. Once the hold position is set up, the eyes must be allowed just to look out in the general area and the target called.

# Shooting method

Shooting Olympic Trap involves the use of the classic 'swing-through' method. This is the only sane way to shoot any Trap discipline, since the target is aways going away from the gun before it is seen.

At address, the shooter's weight should favour the forward foot and this bias increases as the shooter goes for the target. For many OT shooters the weight transference will mean that most of their weight goes onto the forward foot, with the heel of the rear foot raised from the ground, this foot merely serving to retain balance. At no time should the shooter have his weight on his rear foot as this will bind the swing to the point that it is impossible to bring the gun to bear on the target.

Regardless of the angle or height of the target, the approach is exactly the same. The muzzles follow the target flightline and ultimately catch the target and pass it. Depending on the target, the shot is fired as or just after the target is passed.

Some shooters feel that they give a certain amount of forward allowance on the wider angled targets, while others feel that they shoot the instant the gun is brought to bear on the target itself. It is highly unlikely that even the most lead-conscious shooter will see much forward allowance: the speed of the swing removes the need. There is a slight delay between the subconscious saying 'pull the trigger' and the finger actually pulling it, and this delay is sufficient to give enough automatic lead to break most trap targets.

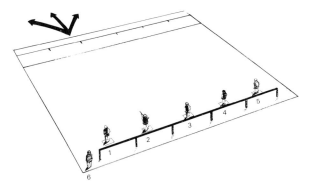

Squad of six shooting Olympic Trap.

It should be noted that, as in all forms of shotgun shooting, the act of getting the muzzles to catch and pass the target involves a body turn as well as an arm and hand movement. This is why stance and foot position are so important to the outcome of each shot. Training as suggested in Training Methods (see page 132) will help this.

Of all the various suggestions and pieces of advice which are offered throughout the book, the most important applies just as much to Olympic Trap as it does to all the other disciplines: focus the eyes on the target! This has been repeated many times and for good reason: it is the main element without which the whole procedure crumbles. The shooter's first concern must be to get the target focused as quickly as possible because only then can an accurate and smooth shot be executed. To swing after a hazy, ill-defined blob rapidly heading to the outfield is going to result in a hazy and ill-defined shot.

Particularly in the case of the international disciplines, with their emphasis on fast targets, the shooter must always be 'battle ready' when calling for his target and, in a good mental state, his eyes will fasten immediately on to the target as it emerges.

In this condition the OT shooter will take his targets quickly and smoothly, but not necessarily because he is moving any faster (although he probably will be): by focusing the target quickly, he is able to start *earlier* and thereby catch the target sooner.

## Using the second barrel

One of the problems concerning Trap shooters is the amount of barrel disturbance caused by the first shot. Depending on the shape of the stock the barrels do several things when a shot is fired. The whole gun moves back (recoil) as the cartridge explodes, but the barrels also move upwards as well as sometimes to the side, especially if the gun has a considerable amount of cast-off or cast-on.

All other factors being equal, the higher the centre of the fired barrel is above the main point that the stock beds in the shoulder, the more the muzzles will deflect upwards. Therefore, the trigger selector should always be set so that the lower barrel fires first, never the other way round.

Having sorted this out, the next concern is the actual firing of the second shot.

In the case of Olympic Trap, most shooters manage to get their first shot fired when the target is between 30-35 yards away, although the low, wider targets are often taken somewhat later. Allowing for the shooter's instinctive correction of the muzzle deflection, it means that the second barrel is often being fired when the target is at a range of 40 yards and more.

Because a carefully aimed shot is out of the question, the second barrel has to be fired completely reflexively, without thought, the guidance system relying entirely on the result of hand and eye co-ordination. This means that the time lag between the two shots is considerably less than would be normal for, say, a sporting double.

Training the reflexes to handle good second barrel shooting is achieved simply by firing plenty of second barrel shots. It also entails shooting at the bits of broken clay when the target is hit with the first barrel. This practice may seem an awful waste of cartridges but, in fact, for most international Trapshooters it is an essential part of their shooting technique. An OT shooter is only as good as the effectiveness of his second barrel, and the only way to maintain it in fighting trim is to keep firing it!

This is particularly vital when the shooter is having a purple patch and breaking all his targets first barrel. If he does not keep himself 'second barrel fit' throughout each round, by constantly using it on the flying pieces of his broken clays, he may find that when the moment comes when he *has* to use that second barrel he will hesitate for a fatal split second and the target will be gone.

While aesthetically it may be more satisfactory to break 24 targets with the first barrel with one missed completely, the practical Trapshooter will settle for 25 straight breaks even if it means 15 of them were gathered up by the second barrel!

## Targets which emerge broken

Frequently, the shooter will call for his target only to have it come out in pieces. Unless the target goes to dust, the flying bits show which way the target would have gone had it not broken. The shooter waits for the referee to indicate that the trap has been re-loaded, then he sets himself up and calls for it again.

Theoretically, the shooter should get the same target again but, contrary to what the layman might think, this is no advantage at all. The shooter must try to ignore the fact that he knows which way his target will be heading. If he does not, he may well start to move in that direction before the target actually appears, which will tend to disrupt his natural timing. Much worse than this, he might not actually *get* the same target again. The outcome of starting to move to the left on a target that actually goes to the right does not take much figuring out. Unfortunately, although such an occurrence is wrong, as a result of which the shooter will get an incorrect target distribution, the wrong target is still 'legal' and the shooter has no redress should he miss it.

### Training

Most of what is included in Training Methods applies to Olympic Trap. However, there is no getting away from the fact that, probably even more than with Skeet or Sporting, actual regular shooting practice is essential to the development of the necessary skills.

I personally learned a great deal of my Skeet shooting technique through much repeated 'dry practice', good robot-like movement being much of what top level Skeet shooting is all about. I do not think the same approach would work as well with such a reflex-based discipline as Olympic Trap.

US shooters in training for Olympic Trap. Small shelters are for sun, not rain!

## In conclusion

This discipline is without doubt the ultimate test of Trapshooting skill and I can only say that any Trapshooter who has not given it a try is missing out on one of the best clay shooting games of them all. Why not have a go and see?

# 10
## Training
## Methods

One of the attractions of all the shooting disciplines is the fact that it is possible for a top-level competitor to continue producing the very highest performance well into middle age and beyond, something possibly unique in world-class sport.

In most other sports there is a trade-off: as experience and knowledge increase, physical abilities decline to a point at which the body is no longer capable of producing a high-level performance. In gymnastics, for instance, demands on the body are so intense that most competitors are finished with international competition by the time they are in their twenties, while most athletes are taking part for fun by the time they reach their thirties. Shooters, however, are frequently just beginning to make their mark in their mid-thirties, and world championships have been won by shooters the 'wrong' side of forty-five.

It has often been said that success in shooting is mainly between the ears but, while this is probably true for those who have already attained a high level of performance, it does not apply to the aspiring international and certainly not to the newcomer. Hand and eye co-ordination and good reflexes are attributes possessed by most people, but it is only through a sensible training routine that these can be harnessed and put to work for the shooter striving to succeed.

## Physical fitness

As neither great strength nor explosive movement are requirements of any type of clay shooting, training with weights is of doubtful benefit. More relevant are activities such as squash, badminton, tennis, etc., which, while creating a high level of general physical fitness, also constantly exercise those two vital ingredients of top-level clay shooting: reflexes and co-ordination.

Physical conditioning might seem a strange thing to recommend for a sport so apparently lacking in any form of actual exertion but in a long shoot, which can last three or four days, tiredness, both physical and mental, is a constant factor to be overcome.

Without doubt, a competitor in first-class physical condition will survive such a marathon much better than will those who are out of shape.

131

## Shooting training

Nothing can substitute for actual shooting practice but there are a number of training methods which can be employed to complement work done on the shooting ground.

During the average practice session, the number of times the gun is mounted is probably less than 200. As the shooter's attention is likely to be totally on the targets during such sessions, and quite rightly, it is obvious that the amount of time spent on observing actual technique is probably minimal. For this reason it can be beneficial to practise basic technique away from the shooting range, when full attention can be applied to such things as gunmount, balanced movement, stance, etc. Regular gunmounting practice is particularly recommended for Sporting and ISU skeet, where incorrect gunmounting is responsible for many missed targets.

All that is needed for this practice is a small amount of space, the gun, and a full-length mirror. The mirror is to check the gunmount position and the movement which precedes it, something which cannot be checked by feel alone.

Since it is important that everything should be as it is when actually shooting, it is essential to wear whatever shooting clothing is usually worn at the shooting ground. Then the method is as follows.

First of all the shooter positions himself so that the mirror is on his gun side and he is standing facing obliquely across the mirror.

With the gun in the ready position and the shooter in a comfortable stance, the leading hand pushes the gun towards an imagined target as the other hand pushes and raises the gun up to the cheek. No discernible head movement should occur as the gun is being mounted, the only permissible movement being a slight transference of weight onto the leading foot. The mirror is then checked to examine the finished position. Something which will not happen automatically is a slight hunching forward of the shoulder as the gun comes into position. This performs two important functions. One is that the gun is mounted without recourse to any pulling back of the stock to the shoulder, a movement which can upset the line of the barrels during a shot, and the other is that the hunched shoulder creates a solid bed for the gun stock, thus assuring its location during recoil as well as helping absorb the impact of the shot. The position can easily be seen with the mirror.

The complete movement should be carried out slowly at first, always checking the gunmount before taking the gun back to the ready position. One point worth noting here is that most people practise their gunmounting at a speed usually much greater than they ever need when actually shooting. A slow practice mount, then, will seem very slow. What is ultimately intended is that the shooter makes a steady, controlled movement even when shooting the fastest targets.

Once the correct gunmount can be achieved at this slow speed the tempo can be gradually increased until the gun is being mounted at normal speed—which, remember, is not fast.

It takes surprisingly few gunmounts before the practice becomes tiring.

Try this:

1 Adopt the correct stance and ready position. Slowly mount the gun and maintain the position for a count of five seconds, taking care not to allow the gun or arms to droop!
2 Lower the gun and repeat 1.
3 Repeat the sequence twenty-five times, gradually increasing the speed of mount to normal but not decreasing the position-hold time.
4 Rest for 30 seconds.
5 Repeat 1-4 twice more.
6 Stop altogether for a period of continued rest.

Many shooters surprise themselves when they try this exercise. Most get through the first sequence with some sort of struggle. Many burn out halfway through the second sequence, while a very small minority make it right through to the end. However, until a shooter can get through these sequences without collapsing, he can hardly consider himself to be in good shooting condition!

For ladies, training with this sequence or something similar is essential, as they tend to have less natural strength than men and yet must use guns which are relatively heavy if the recoil level is to remain tolerable.

For both men and women, as fatigue sets in so technique begins to crumble and these exercises will go some way towards avoiding that. Having tried a variety of weight-assisted exercises, I can't say I've found anything as good as working with the actual gun. All the right muscles are being trained and a great deal of familiarity with the gun is acquired at the same time.

Again, with Skeet and Sporting primarily in mind, the same sequence of movements should be attempted while swinging to left and right. This is not simply a matter of mounting the gun and then swinging. Such a movement is a fundamental error which will allow the target to get away from the gun as the gun is being raised to the shoulder. The correct movement involves turning and mounting the gun in one co-ordinated movement, not as two separate movements.

It is equally bad to move the gun to the target, with the body remaining stationary. The result is that the gun is dragged across the body when swinging to the left, and away from the face when swinging to the right (other way round for left-handers, of course).

To repeat, the correct movement is to turn the body and mount the gun in one united movement, not two separate ones.

With Sporting shooters in mind, the same type of movement can be practised on imaginary overhead targets, making sure that the gun muzzles move upwards *as* the gun is being mounted, *not* after.

Care must be exercised during these practices to ensure that form remains correct. In the early stages fatigue will set in surprisingly quickly and it is then best to stop. To practise bad form is worse than no practice at all.

Once the shooter can easily sustain this physical practice without undue fatigue, he can move on a stage further.

## The visualisation technique

The imagination is a faculty used by all of us, particularly those involved in any sort of creative work, and it is just this ability to conjure up images in our minds that can be used—in conjunction with the gunmounting practice just described—as an aid to better shooting.

What is needed is a quiet room, preferably darkened, and a certain amount of single-minded application. The reason for the darkened room is to avoid the possibility of becoming too conscious of the barrels during the practice.

The Skeet shooter then shoots, in his mind, a round of Skeet, the Trap shooter a round of Trap, while the Sporting shooter can decide on any one of a number of different possibilities.

What this entails is straightforward enough, at least in theory. The shooter takes himself through an imaginary round of Trap, Skeet or Sporting, positioning himself on each 'station', calling for each target (or targets) and 'shooting' each of the imaginary targets with full concentration, ideally 'seeing' them break as he does so.

In actual practice this is far more difficult than it sounds. All manner of extraneous thoughts intrude to disrupt the visualisation process, just the sort of unwanted diversions which occur when actually shooting. Even when the practice is undertaken in total solitude, it is amazing how many unwanted thoughts will keep occurring. However, with constant practice the shooter will find that a cocoon of concentration gradually builds up which will allow him to concentrate fully for that few vital seconds when he takes his position on the imaginary stand, calls for the target and shoots it.

Once the shooter is able to do this fairly successfully, it will begin to have an effect when shooting the real thing; it will be of great assistance during actual shooting-training and competition.

It must be stressed again that both the gunmount practice and its extension, the visualisation technique, cannot stand alone as methods of improving one's shooting. They are meant to be complementary to, and not a replacement for, actual shooting on real targets. Furthermore, the suggested method of visualisation falls well short of some of the techniques advised in a more learned treatise, but deliberately so.

Anything more advanced than this somewhat rustic version of the visualisation method is beyond the scope of this book (and its writer!) It is just as well, since many writers on the subject seem to forget that they are dealing with sportsmen and women, most of whom have limited time and even less interest in fanciful theorising. It is only too easy for the shooter to lose sight of what he is actually trying to achieve, with the result that he gets worse instead of better!

However, used sensibly in conjunction with sessions at the shooting ground, these techniques can prove a very powerful aid to dramatic score improvement.

## Shooting practice

As has already been mentioned, no matter how much dry practice is done there can be no substitute for actual shooting.

For many shooters, practice means a relaxing period when targets are shot in a fairly casual fashion, usually with friends and others of like mind. It can be a very enjoyable way to pass a few hours and something most shooters do from time to time. However, for the shooter with serious aspirations, such an approach is unproductive, possibly even retrogressive and certainly a waste of time and cash.

Anyone who thinks that this is rather a joyless attitude towards what is for most shooters an enjoyable game, must bear in mind that many sportsmen obtain great satisfaction from devoting themselves completely to getting as near perfection as is possible in their chosen sport. Top shooters are no different.

Very few of the top shooters in any given discipline have more than a passing interest in any other sport or pastime. In other words, they tend to specialise and if this specialisation is going to have any meaning at all then the discipline concerned must be approached at all times with serious intent.

There are a few who, after a poor performance, may shrug their shoulders indifferently and say, 'Oh well, I only do it for fun anyway'. The single-minded specialist does not offer this excuse, at least not when shooting his own discipline. If he really fancies doing some shooting for fun, which even the most dedicated must do at times, it is best to do it away from the area of specialisation. He can go and shoot another discipline where the results do not matter too much, although the dedicated competitor will probably find he is forced to give even this his best attention. But he would be better advised to go and play one of the competitive racquet games and sharpen up the reflexes at the same time.

Serious shooting practice has several intentions: improvement in technique or maintaining an already high standard; correction of errors on any problem targets; maintaining a high score average; and development of the right attitude so that these scores may be reproduced under competition conditions.

Although the last two are closely related, it is possible for shooters to be good in practice but poor performers in competition. This may be the result of practising in too convivial an atmosphere. When results are of no concern, it is quite possible to produce good scores with a method that is a little suspect, but under competition pressure these errors are magnified—and down goes the score.

Practice is never worthwhile under light-hearted conditions. Shoot with friends if you must, but shoot 'a tenner' each on the outcome. That will keep everyone serious!

## Handling problem shots

Error correction is difficult without assistance, for the simple reason that the shooter cannot stand back and take an objective view of himself. A video camera might help to point out a glaring error, such as a bad stance or gunmount, but beyond this it takes the discerning eye of an experienced shooter or, better still, a good coach.

There are a fair number of coaches available for the Sporting shooter, but the Trap or Skeet shooter will have to search hard to find someone who is very expert, particularly as far as the international disciplines are concerned. Plenty of people can tell you where you have missed a target, but that is only the effect and not the cause of the problem. If a shooting coach is not available, a fellow shooter who really knows your normal style can help, but remember that a good shot is not necessarily a good coach.

If none of these alternatives is feasible, then resort to correction through dry practice. Instead of worrying about what not to do, concentrate on the application of correct technique. Frequently, it will be found that the problem is something simple, like a stance error or poor weight distribution.

A troublesome target is sometimes the result of a mental block. A shooter finds that he can shoot every other target perfectly well but he fails consistently on one bird. Again, concentrate on *what* to do, not on what *not* to do. Applying the right technique, while temporarily disregarding the result, is often a good way to overcome this sort of problem. One word of advice. *Never* tell anyone that you are having trouble with a particular target. There are those who will not hesitate to remind you of the fact, even when you have at last got it straightened out in your mind. This does not help at all. Keep it to yourself.

Striving to maintain a high practice-score average is one way of guaranteeing that every session is a serious one. The newcomer, who obviously has no score at all, must shoot a series of scores over a period of some weeks. From this he will find his average score.

The next step is to set a realistic goal at which to aim. For instance, if the shooter finds he has averaged 75% over six sessions, he can set himself a realistic goal of 78% over the next six. It will put a degree of pressure on the shooter and, as the scores gradually rise, so the goal can be set that much higher. Obviously, once a certain level has been attained, specially if it is a fairly high one, the shooter will have his work cut out just trying to maintain the standard that he has set for himself.

Because competition will always contain elements not present during practice, it is reasonable just to try maintaining the practice average, and not to improve upon it. If you can do this, you are on your way to becoming a good competitor.

The right attitude will come through correct practice of sound technique, both in training and competition. Once the shooter can automatically adopt a serious, concentrated approach whenever he shoots, in practice or competition, he will be well on the way to developing a mental toughness, and this is the finest attribute any competitor can possess.

# 11

## Competition Shooting

The satisfaction to be derived from the breaking of a small and distant flying disc is probably rather difficult for the layman to appreciate; that is, until he or she actually tries it.

For those unfamiliar with firearms it can often be quite an experience just to shoot a 'real' gun, but if the gun can also be directed at a flying target which is knocked out of the sky, then the wonder is complete and another clay shooter is born.

While all of us retain this feeling to some extent, the beginner's initial satisfaction, gained from breaking the occasional target, soon changes to a strong desire to break them all. The shooter is then only a short step away from wanting to hit more than his friends can.

The readiness to compete is strong in most men and many women, and one of the great attractions of clay shooting is that competition shooting of one sort or another is very available at whatever level one chooses to take part.

Unlike most other sports, clay competitions up to national standard are open to all comers, the class system ensuring that while one of the top shooters will almost inevitably come out the winner, this group cannot take all the money!

### Learning to compete

The idea that competing is something which has to be learned may sound odd to the casual reader, but anyone who has competed at any sport with serious intent will know that it is one thing having talent and quite another when you have to prove it in competition!

Competition can do strange things to people. Rational men or women can find themselves trembling at the thought of shooting in a twenty-five target shoot at their local club and may well do so every time it is their turn to shoot. They need feel no shame, for they are in good company. Show me a shooter at a World Championships who is not nervous and I will show you a shooter who is not going to win!

The *degree* of nervousness is what separates the top shooters from the rest of the crowd, however. The top shooter's nervousness is controlled and in this condition he is fully alert and ready to go, his reflexes and eyesight tuned to maximum pitch.

'Tuned eyesight' is perhaps the wrong expression, but I cannot think of a better one. When the shooter is properly keyed up and in charge

138

of his emotions he really will see better and his reflexes will be that much sharper.

Control like this is something which only comes with plenty of experience, as well as a willingness to jump in at the deep end. The shooter who sticks to his or her twenty-five target competitions will probably always be too nervous when taking part in them and this is no good. Just as the right level of nervousness can enhance a shooter's performance, so an excess of nerves can have quite the opposite effect.

The answer is to try always to go up a grade. Try to shoot in, say, a fifty target competition where the top competitors are of a higher standard than those usually encountered. The first outing to such a shoot may well be a frightening experience, but this feeling soon wears off. Once a few of these have been endured the old twenty-five target shoot, if retried, will seem relatively easy.

Following this sort of progression the shooter will eventually arrive at shoots of national level, and even these can be taken in one's stride after a while. Of course, it may be further than many shooters are intending to go, but for them, the principle still applies.

## The competitor

By definition a competitor is someone who takes part in a competition, but there is a world of difference between someone who competes for fun and the person who competes with intent. It is from the latter group that the winners inevitably emerge.

It is often evident that in the minds and bodies of many of those who supposedly shoot 'for fun' there is a frustrated competitor bursting to get out, but he does not know how.

Many shooters suffer from a fear of failure and get around it by pretending to themselves that it does not really matter how they shoot because, after all, they are only there for a bit of fun. The shooter who comes off the Skeet range, laughing at having just missed his last target for twenty-five straight, is a good example. It may have been the closest he has been to shooting a 'straight' for months, but the laugh lets everyone around him know that he does not really care. Strangely, his laughter has a rather hollow ring. Unfortunately, this careful camouflaging of the shooter's real feelings is very restrictive because it means that he will always shoot at a frivolous level and is permanently held back by his reluctance to be seen to be really trying!

The real competitor is one who always gives maximum effort, win or lose, and he never gives up. He will not come off the range with a smile on his face having just missed his last target. In fact, in many cases, such a shooter may well be unapproachable until the internal steam has backed off, and he has returned to a calmer condition.

Obviously, not everyone can be the winner: there is only one first place in any competition and apart from that rarity, the unbroken tie, only one person can fill it. However, being a winner is more about attitude than eventual placing in a competition. Very often the serious competitor will find that despite his best efforts he is not going to win because he just has not shot well enough. As has been said, there is only one winner. However, if the shooter cannot win, he can look to come second, third, fourth or whatever. If none of these positions is achievable, then he must look to preserve as good a score as possible, even if it means barely scraping into the first fifty places!

## Competition

Successful competition shooting requires a number of things besides those already touched upon. While the right attitude is very necessary, it is not the only weapon in the good shooter's armoury.

Probably the most obvious attribute is a certain amount of basic talent without which even the most dedicated shooter is wasting his time. However, very few people indeed have no shooting talent whatsoever and with effort a little can go a long way.

The next thing the aspiring competitor needs to acquire is knowledge: knowledge of his chosen discipline, its rules and unique requirements as well as knowledge of his gun and equipment. This can be assimilated by talking to those who have a great deal of expertise (if he can get them to talk, that is!); reading anything he can find on the discipline; and actual experience (the best teacher of all). Behind even the most bland of the top shooters there is a depth of knowledge, often much more than most people would ever expect or believe.

Take my word for it, the shooters who are regularly successful know exactly what they are doing and have put much thought into it. This gives them yet another tiny but important edge over those who do not bother.

Given the right attitude and knowledge, the next step is correct training. This is covered elsewhere under Training Methods (see page 133). It is worth re-iterating here, though, that training and correct training need not be the same thing. The right attitude in training is just as important as in actual competition, because casual training sessions lead nowhere and may even be harmful. So train as you mean to compete: with serious intent.

## Psychology

There was a lot of talk a few years ago regarding the possible value of sports psychology techniques to clay shooting. It was thought that if a shooter could learn to adjust his heart rate and gain control over his emotional condition during competition, he would have a definite advantage over those not trained in this way.

A number of experiments were carried out, culminating in a study group being formed, comprised of British ISU Skeet shooters. The group undertook a course of 'Autogenic Training', a series of techniques originally devised to assist the recovery of mentally ill patients. This particular form of mental training had previously been successfully employed by British rifle shooters.

It would be nice to report that at the end of their training the group improved, but unfortunately all, without exception, suffered a noticeable loss of form, something from which several never really recovered.

The main error seemed to lay not with the 'Autogenic' form of training but rather with the psychologists' lack of understanding of the requirements of ISU Skeet. The sort of mental approach that will bring under control a totally static rifle shooter firing at a completely immobile target is not likely to work well in a sport like ISU skeet, where the emphasis is on fast reflexes and quick movement. It would seem, therefore, that the psychological approach on which one sport thrives will possibly sound the death knell for another sport which is totally dissimilar.

Continuing that theme, a psychologist would probably need a thorough working knowledge of a given sport before he could proceed to teach any form of mental training: a passing interest would hardly suffice. In clay shooting, and in many other sports I suspect, psychologists with such insight are somewhat thin on the ground.

To my mind, and those of many others, this little experiment underlined the dangers of dabbling in areas where even the most knowledgeable are barely beginning to scratch the surface. Considerable work has been done in this field, however, and no doubt there are sportsmen and women who have benefitted as a result. Nevertheless, one of the great dangers of the modern emphasis on mental training is that the individual sportsman or woman becomes obsessed with the subject to the detriment of his or her physical training. If employed at all, specific mental training should be regarded as the icing on the cake, a factor which may assist a top competitor to reach the pinnacle of performance. I doubt it would benefit those still struggling to master the basic physical techniques of their respective sports.

Until psychologists finally discover what makes us all tick I shall continue to subscribe to the idea that most worthwhile clay shooting training involves the use of the gun, and that the most beneficial training involves actually firing it, too!

# Index